Ex Líbrís

ALSO BY KENNETH LO:

Chinese Regional Cooking
Chinese Cooking on Next to Nothing
Chinese Vegetarian Cooking
Peking Cooking

# NEW
# CHINESE
# VEGETARIAN
# COOKING

# NEW CHINESE VEGETARIAN COOKING

## KENNETH LO

Pantheon Books New York

Library of Congress Cataloging-in-Publication Data

Lo, Kenneth H. C.
New Chinese vegetarian cooking.
Includes index.
1. Vegetarian cookery.   2. Cookery, Chinese.
I. Title.
TX837.L56   1987      641.5'636'0951      86-16979
ISBN 0-394-75005-5

Book design by Guenet Abraham

Manufactured in the United States of America

First American Edition

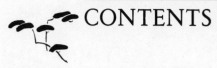 CONTENTS

INTRODUCTION 3

## 4 RICE 105

## 5 SOUPS 129

## 6 NOODLES 145

## 7 STEAMED BUNS, DUMPLINGS, AND PANCAKES 166

## 8 FRUIT, NUTS, AND FLOWERS 180

## INDEX 197

# NEW
# CHINESE
# VEGETARIAN
# COOKING

# INTRODUCTION

The recent drift away from meat-eating and meat cookery toward vegetable-eating and vegetable cookery is becoming more and more apparent in the affluent West. This can be put down to the natural swing of the pendulum; the fact that too much importance was attached to meat-eating and cookery in the past, and too little to cooking and eating vegetables. Traditionally, vegetables have been treated only as a supplement to meat by the rich, while poor people and peasants could rarely afford to eat meat (except for the game they caught) and therefore had to survive on roots and vegetables. Now, an English friend of mine tells me, it is the wealthy who are turning vegetarian.

During the nineteenth century and the first half of the twentieth, a period of unprecedented economic growth and expansion, the West—characteristically in a hurry—never took the trouble to explore all the avenues of creative cookery. Whatever opportunity there may have been was wasted in harking back to the glorious Empire days of French cuisine, which concentrated on creating sauces to accompany meat and vegetables rather than on developing the flavors of the foods themselves. More recently, the mass production of beef, lamb, and chicken in Australasia, the United States, and Argentina has encouraged an excessive consumption of meat—another reason why the art of cooking vegetables has not been properly developed in the West.

It is only in the last couple of decades that the West has become aware of and begun to appreciate the range of cookery traditions and practices that exists on the other continents of the world. Interest in ethnic cooking is currently booming, with Indian and Chinese cuisines probably being the most popular—and these are, of course, mainly vegetable and cereal based. This new interest seems to have encouraged a fresh Western interest in vegetable cookery.

It is also true to say that the Western disillusionment with and loss of interest in meat has stemmed from the constant overuse of meat in the average meal, and from not allowing vegetables to be integrally incorporated into meat dishes. This limits the number of meat (or primarily meat) dishes that can be produced; but, in Chinese "compound cookery," for example, where meats and vegetables *are* often incorporated together in the same dish, the number of dishes that can be created is truly unlimited. Hence with Chinese food and cooking there is as yet very little apparent drift from meat to vegetable cookery, partly because there is much more middle ground between meat and vegetable cookery in China; and partly because urbanization and industrialization are only very recent phenomena in China, and the country has not yet reached the standard of living where meat is eaten in such quantities that people have begun to get bored with it. On the contrary, over 90 percent of the Chinese population still lives off the land and much of the time subsists almost entirely on cereals and vegetables. Indeed, in the majority of Chinese households meat is only served occasionally, maybe no more than once or twice a month. The rest of the time the Chinese have to make do with largely meatless meals, and to look forward to special occasions when a pig might be slaughtered or a chicken killed to celebrate a wedding, birthday, memorial, anniversary, or festival. China today still strives towards enabling the bulk of the population to eat more meat of all types, rather than less.

Where Chinese cookery can contribute to the Western interest in vegetarian cooking lies primarily in its ability to draw upon the immense resources and experience of the peasantry of China, who are largely vegetarian. Secondly, it draws upon the Buddhist influence, which has been fairly prominent throughout all levels of Chinese society over the centuries. Vegetarianism in the past was centered largely around the Buddhist monasteries and temples. There were temples in most large villages or small townships, and monasteries of different sizes were scattered throughout the provinces of China.

Although Buddhism is not and never has been a state religion in China, because it is inextricably involved with Confucianism and Taoism in the Chinese subconscious and in the Chinese striving to find comfort and an explanation for man's place in this universe, its influence is broader than its official establishments. Many Chinese practice Buddhism even if not officially affiliated to any Buddhist organization, and because they are partially Buddhist, they are also at least partially vegetarian. Since freedom of belief is enshrined in the Chinese constitution, and a majority of temples and monasteries are nowadays being vigorously restored to their former often-garish glory, I imagine much of Buddhism and its vegetarian practices have survived the rigors of revolution and the devastation by the Cultural Revolution. Indeed, my feeling is that, in general, Chinese Buddhist vegetarian cooks today are only just beginning to find their feet again, have had too little time to find a new bearing, and are mostly inclined to hark back to the past. Many of the exploitable territories are still waiting to be explored—like much of China's heritage as it comes into contact with the forward momentum of development taking place in the Western world.

Chinese cooking is likely to make its major contribution to Western vegetarian interest in the areas of culinary technique and the use of ingredients. Although the basic foods used in China—cereals and vegetables—are much the same as the familiar foods consumed in the West, the flavoring of ingredients and the cooking methods employed derive from entirely different traditions. There should therefore be vast scope for adaptation and innovation using Chinese methods and ingredients to produce dishes that are acceptable and appealing to the average Western palate.

The principal methods of Chinese cooking are those with which the West is not completely familiar. Methods that we Chinese use practically all the time are steaming and stir-frying. Soybean products and by-products are used extensively to flavor both vegetarian and other foods, and we also use more ingredients which have been pickled, salted, dried, and spiced to flavor in particular bulk foods than is customary in the West. In creating and generating taste, we rely more heavily on coating ingredients with hot flavored and seasoned oil as a way of spreading the flavor from the stronger-tasting foods to the neutral and blander foods, or to merge the seasoned and matured flavor with the sweet and fresh.

Furthermore, we are much more in the habit of cross-cooking different ingredients, which results in the greater blending not only of flavors but also of textures and colors. Thus many more dishes can be created than would be possible if one were confined to simple cooking, as is the normal practice in the West. Chinese cross-cooking is achieved by cutting food materials into small pieces, whether shreds, thin slices, or cubes, which enables them to be stirred or tossed together at different temperatures with greater ease. A variety of sauces and ingredients can be added as you go along for flavoring. Cross-cooking applies not only to mixing different raw food materials but also to mingling well-cooked and seasoned ingredients with fresh, uncooked food materials.

This practice of cross-cooking actually opens up innumerable avenues for the creative and enterprising chef. Although the Chinese chef is as much bound by tradition and conventional practice as the classic Western chef, he is probably accorded greater freedom of "interpretation" because of the sheer complexity of Chinese cooking and the numerous options open to him at each stage of the process. This applies as much to vegetarian as to nonvegetarian cooking. Chinese recipes are seldom meant to be adhered to completely; they are written down more as guidelines for interested parties to follow and to make their own interpretations.

This brings us to the presentation of foods and dishes. Chinese cookery has a great advantage over *nouvelle cuisine*, whose practitioners aim to produce small, light dishes, and therefore project postcard-size representations of the food they create and serve. The Chinese do not have such restrictions. Indeed, because Chinese dishes are usually created and cooked for half a dozen to a dozen people, they are usually conceived on a much larger scale. Instead of always aiming to produce small-sized dishes, with their obvious limitations, the Chinese have a much freer rein. This can often lead to results comparable to landscape gardening, in which some parts of the garden may be intricately and delicately designed in miniature, while other parts are allowed to grow wild. There is therefore much more scope for the practice of "art to conceal art," resulting in more impressive effects. Consequently, Chinese cooking is likely to be much nearer to the ideals of *cuisine naturelle* than of *nouvelle cuisine* insofar as it endeavors to project not only the natural appearance of foods but also their natural flavor and characteristics. Nowadays these are often lost through overzealous attempts to create man-made designs and to compress them into small spaces.

I should explain that what I am mostly concerned with in this book is not the classical vegetarian cuisine of China, which often has its limitations. Traditionally, it is much too inclined to produce imitations of meat dishes, such as "vegetarian duck," "vegetarian goose," "vegetarian fish," and so on, as if vegetables were able to hold their ground only if they resemble meat. Indeed, classic vegetarian cooks sometimes succeed in achieving a remarkable likeness to meat, for which they deserve our applause, but in such endeavors they sacrifice much of their energy and creativeness, which could otherwise be devoted to bringing out the true assets and qualities of the vegetables themselves.

What I should like to do here is to bring about a renaissance of the vegetables themselves, in relation to the satisfaction and appeal they can have for the human palate and other senses through their flavor or their other essential qualities, such as texture, aroma, color, or shape, by applying to them the Chinese techniques of cutting, flavor-blending, and heat control in cooking, and the use of supplementary materials and ingredients peculiar to Chinese cooking traditions. Some of these should help to add a new dimension to vegetarian food and vegetable cookery, which, whether they are practiced in the East or the West, are going through a period of considerable transformation.

In the past people have been content to imitate the classics. As more and more attention has been brought to bear on this, the past has often been found wanting. This has spurred many knowledgeable people on to explore new territories and make greater use of their own creative instincts. Few of us who have gained an acquaintance with the greatness of the classics are satisfied just to sit still and worship the past. The world is always evolving and, whether in art, architecture, or literature, every age must bring forth its new forms and concepts. Painting did not stop with the French Impressionists, nor architecture with Wren, nor landscape gardening with Capability Brown, nor literature with Dickens. Thackeray, or the Lake Poets, great though they may have been. Every artist who has any spark of creativeness is groping his or her way forward. Nowhere is this truer than in the world of cookery. With cookbooks nowadays overflowing the bookshelves, cookery writers and chefs all over the world must indeed work overtime to break new ground.

Yet to initiate a culinary revolution, or at least to start a new trend, requires inspiration. It said that the French were inspired by the subtler Oriental approach when they embarked on their *nouvelle cuisine*. Within a very few years, however, they have become aware of the failings and limitations of this style of cooking, in which visual effects are often achieved at the expense of flavor generation and flavor-blending. Western cooks, now experiencing the staleness that results from excessive devotion to design without the corresponding development of flavor, are rapidly drifting away from *nouvelle cuisine* in search of new pastures, and could be heading towards *cuisine naturelle*. Whatever its direction, it will require a degree of inspiration to put the next trend on course. Usually when the world's cooks are at a loss for inspiration, they revert to their roots. In France, for example, this means going back to their "bourgeois" cooking, their *cuisine paysanne*, their *cuisine régionale*, and their established classics, which are, after all, the bulk and mainstay of their national culinary heritage.

In China today, because of the lapse in culinary development and interest since the revolution of 1949, and especially during the decade of the Cultural Revolution of the 1960s, the country is making a conscious effort to catch up with the past. Innumerable cooking schools seem to have been established in every province in the country to speed up this process. Since their culinary heritage is a vast one, some time will elapse before the Chinese will feel the need to explore new ground. However, once the interest in food and cooking is rekindled, there are bound to be people who will experiment and find new ways of doing things. It is therefore likely that the "new wave" in Chinese cooking will generate its first ripples and gradually gather momentum while it is still engaged in the process of rediscovering the past.

During this period of innovation, Chinese cooking is likely to find its greatest inspiration in its contact with the West, coupled with the rediscovery of China's past and the vastness of its own resources. The influence of the West in culinary matters, as in all aspects of our activities, is likely to be felt all along the line. However, it should be pointed out that in cultural matters we Chinese have always regarded the Western infuence as something peripheral rather than as touching on the "heart of the matter." Considering the size, weight, and vitality of the Chinese culinary heritage, it is likely that, although Western cooking methods may have a significant impact on it in the future, Chinese cooking should on the whole be able to maintain its completely independent character. In fact, it should be able to contribute more to the world's culinary practices and culture at large than it is able to absorb from the West.

The situation with Chinese vegetarian cooking is similar; the Chinese have much to do to reclaim their own heritage, and the West is likely to influence the future of Chinese vegetarian food and its preparation during this period of rediscovery. Within China itself, as I have said, temples and monasteries are being renovated and rebuilt at some speed, and they will soon become centers not only of tourist interest only again—but of Chinese vegetarian cooking as well. As this process gathers momentum, it should not take the Chinese too long to reacquaint themselves with all their vegetarian classics.

It would be interesting to know the directions in which Chinese vegetarian cooking is likely to move from now on. As I see it, the one way in which it could profitably develop is to incorporate more fruits and flowers. Since some of the principal flavorings of Chinese food (vegetarian and nonvegetarian) are soy based—soy sauce, soy paste, bean curd "cheese"—and since nearly all soy-based ingredients combine well with sugar or honey for their own savory enrichment (a practice little used in Western cuisine), the majority of fruits, having a high sugar content, should also be capable of enhancing the richness and savoriness of vegetarian dishes cooked with soy-based flavoring ingredients. In meat cookery, where more experimentation has been carried out than in vegetarian cooking, dishes such as beef and mango or shredded beef quick-fried with shredded pear have already proved very successful, and these have both been cooked with soy-based marinades. There is no doubt that dates or dried figs can be further enriched by the application of a soy-based flavorer and cooked with vegetables or pasta to produce delicious dishes. The addition of cherries or raisins to fried rice, together with salty pickles, is an obvious example of how fruit can be used in a bulk food to produce a dish of savory rather than sweet appeal.

Chinese stir-fry cooking, where ingredients are thinly sliced or cut into small pieces and tossed and stirred together, offers great opportunities for mixing fruits such as apples (fresh or dried), plums, and peaches with vegetables. Perfect specimens of the fruit can be left whole for decorative purposes to heighten the visual appeal. There are many instances where crunchy fruits can be used to vary and improve the textural interest of a dish, something which, up until now, was normally limited in Chinese cooking to water chestnuts and bamboo shoots.

The use of flowers has long been a tradition in Chinese cooking. A typical dish is the well-known chrysanthemum hotpot, which gets its name partly from the chrysanthemum petals that garnish its top and partly from the chrysanthemum shape of the flame as it rises and caresses the pot from beneath. All kinds of flower petals—violet, marigold, nasturtium, and rose—can be added to Chinese stir-fried dishes. Selected blooms can of course be left whole and perfect to add to the beauty of the dish. The peony, which is the Chinese national flower, is particularly effective because of its large and sturdy blossom. When bonsai miniature trees are featured together with flower-enhanced and flower-decorated dishes, we shall be entering a new dimension in food presentation. As long as we remember that the flavors of flowers are subtle and can easily be blotted out by the much stronger savors of spices and herbs, there is no danger that our aesthetic effects will be achieved at the expense of culinary satisfaction. We must try always to remember that food is above all for the eating.

Those of us who are involved in cooking are deeply aware that all national cuisines need to break new ground if they are to keep vibrant and alive. I feel that, not least of all, this applies to the cooking of China. I hope that I will be able to encourage you, too, to be adventurous and to experiment on the basis of some of my recipes.

Kenneth Lo
London, June 1985

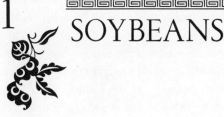

# 1 ﹠ SOYBEANS

One of the most remarkable qualities of the soybean is that it is not only one of the most nutritious foods but is the basis of a number of products highly useful for imparting flavors to other foods. This has made soy sauce one of the principal flavoring agents for foods worldwide, one that is increasingly accepted and used in the West. Ground soybeans, fermented together with flour and salt, subjected to the action of the sun, and combined with a variety of strong-tasting vegetables, are capable of producing a whole range of soy-based products and by-products that can be used not only in cooking but also as table condiments. Gourmets in China can often be heard talking about soy sauces and soy pastes, with all their varieties of flavor, thickness, or strength, in the same knowing manner as Western connoisseurs talk about wines, their vintages, maturities, fruitiness, full-bodiedness, and so on. It is not just a matter of distinguishing between dark soy sauce and light soy sauce (which would be like grading wine as just red or white).

The Japanese have been eating tofu and using miso for flavoring for many hundreds of years, but to the Chinese that is no more than scratching the surface. Soy sauce and soy paste were already being manufactured in China during the millennium before Christ, or before the reign of the first Chinese emperor, Tsing Shi Huang Di. It is interesting to note that these soy products were made not in factories but in "soy gardens" (*jiang yuan*). Presumably, even in those far-off days, soy sauces and soy pastes were made in much the same manner as today. Soybeans and flour are fermented in brine in large, wide-mouthed earthen jars lined up on the ground in a walled garden. The wide mouth of the jar facilitates the action of the sun and the gradual evaporation of the brine, so that the eventual product can be adjusted to different degrees of thickness. Apparently, the Chinese started to use soybean products even before they had discovered the benefits of stir-fry cooking. Before the days of stir-frying, soy products were simply added to meat and vegetable stews, which were cooked together with cereals in large cauldrons called *ding*. With the advent of stir-frying a special form of cooking called *bao* was developed. Meat or root vegetables (or both) are lightly cooked and put to one side. Soy sauce or soy paste is mixed with stock, sugar, wine, and chopped strong-tasting vegetables in a wok or frying pan and reduced to a creamy sauce. The meat or vegetables are returned to the pan or wok for a rapid and second cooking in the bubbling sauce. This method of cooking is still widespread in China today, especially in the north.

One of the most popular forms of Chinese cooking is *shao*, which simply involves stewing the ingredients in stock together with soy sauce, soy paste, and sugar. For more refined cooking, some wine is added. In China stewing with soy sauce is called "red cooking," and most foods can be cooked in this manner, including practically all poultry, meats, and fish, as well as most vegetables. Red cooking is particularly suitable for root vegetables and for harder vegetables such as carrots, eggplants, bamboo shoots, turnips, broccoli, cauliflower, asparagus spears, lotus roots, parsnips, Brussels sprouts, celery, and the harder varieties of cabbage. A whole range of Chinese pickles is brought into full play to enhance or vary the flavor, and in most instances bean curd in its usual form, or dried in the form of skins, sheets, and strips, is added to augment the dish or vary the texture.

Cooking or stewing without soy sauce is termed "white cooking." The harder vegetables are cooked and stewed in vegetarian stock, and bean curd "cheese" is added to achieve richness of flavor. In one form of white cooking, the stock and sauces and dissolved "cheese" are rapidly reduced over high heat to form a mere gloss or coating on the vegetables, which makes the dish extremely tasty. This method is called *kan shao*, or "dry stewing." Ordinary bean curd may be added, or more often dried bean-curd strips or rehydrated bean-curd skins, to cook together with the other vegetable ingredients to produce dishes with a typical Chinese feel and flavor. A spoonful or two of sesame oil may be added to most of these dishes during the very last stage of cooking to enhance their aromatic appeal.

As can clearly be seen from the above, even if we confine ourselves to a few methods of cooking, such as red and white cooking and dry stewing, a considerable range of dishes can be produced without leaving the doorstep of the soybean family. If we also indulge in stir-frying and steaming, as well as several dozen other accepted and well-established methods of Chinese cooking, an even greater number of dishes is available to us. What is intriguing about Chinese cooking is that whenever a new method is introduced and adopted, it immediately opens up fresh avenues, along which a vast number of dishes can be created by varying the permutation of ingredients: the proportions used, the ways they are combined, the order in which they are introduced into the dish. What is remarkable about soybean products and by-products is that somewhere within this process they can usually be put to use either as a principal bulk food or as a flavoring agent. Since the majority of Chinese dishes aim to produce a balance of light, bland, natural flavors with strong, spicy, mature flavors, soybeans in some form are almost invariably called in to play their part, whether in vegetarian or nonvegetarian cooking. The importance of soy products, especially bean curd and soy sauce, in Chinese cooking can hardly be overestimated.

Soy sauce and other soy-based seasoning and flavoring agents are rarely made at home in China, as they are readily available commercially. Bean curd, or tofu, is also usually bought, but it can be made quite easily at home with the help of a blender or food processor. If immersed in water and stored in the refrigerator, it keeps quite well for a week.

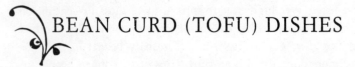

# BEAN CURD (TOFU) DISHES

## TO MAKE BEAN CURD, OR TOFU

One of the simplest ways to make bean curd, or tofu, is as follows. Wash and rinse 1 cup of dried soybeans. Add 1½ cups of water and purée in a blender or food processor. Pour the puree into a saucepan, add 3½ cups of water, bring to a boil, and simmer gently for 15–20 minutes, stirring constantly to prevent burning.

Separate the soy milk by straining the cooked purée through a colander lined with cheesecloth placed over a large saucepan. This should give you about a pint of soy milk for making the bean curd. (The soy mash or pulp that is left over—called *okara* in Japan—is also nutritious and should be reserved for different purposes.) Bring the soy milk quickly to a boil and remove from the heat.

Now stir in a coagulant to curdle the milk. This may consist simply of vinegar or lemon juice—2 or 3 tablespoons to a pint of the milk. Or you may use a solid coagulant such as gypsum, Epsom salts, or one of the Japanese natural solidifiers called Nigari, usually available from Oriental foodstores. For a pint of soy milk, use ½ teaspoon of solid coagulant dissolved in ¼ cup of water. Add the coagulant gradually to the lukewarm milk, stir it well, and let it stand for about 20 minutes.

When the curds have formed and the liquid has become completely clear, the curdled milk should be poured into a specially designed square or oblong wooden box lined with cheesecloth, which will allow the liquid to drain out of the curd. (This liquid should be reserved for other uses.) Allow time for as much of the liquid to drain away as possible.

When this is done, fold the sides of the cloth over the top of the curd in the lined wooden box. A flat wooden lid of the same square or oblong shape, but slightly smaller, which fits inside the top of the box, is then placed on top of the coagulated curd to press it down. A small weight (2–3 pounds) should be placed on top of the lid to provide additional pressure. After 30–45 minutes, when all the liquid has been pressed out, you should have about 4 ounces of bean curd. The heavier the weight, the firmer the bean curd will be.

Since the bean curd is made in a square or oblong box, it comes out in these shapes. It can be cut into halves or quarters or any other convenient size or shape.

To keep, bean curd should be completely immersed in water. If it is kept for more than one day, the water should be changed daily or every other day. If put in a refrigerator, bean curd should keep in good condition for 5–6 days.

Both by-products derived from making bean curd—soy milk (*tou-jiang*) and soy mash (*tou-ja*)—can be used quite independently of bean curd. Soy milk can be drunk in place of dairy milk, and soy mash can be combined with cereals to make bread and pasta, added to meat to make it go further (being much cheaper and just as nutritious), or used as poultry and animal feed.

Once you embark on tofu cookery, you are entering a world in itself. Given the wide variety of Chinese cooking methods and the influence of Western cookery, with its whole range of dairy produce, the number of dishes that can be created using tofu as either the main or a supplementary ingredient is simply limitless.

## BEAN CURD SALAD OR CHINESE COLD-TOSSED BEAN CURD

Since bean curd has already been cooked, it can be served cold without any further cooking or heating. Hence it is a favorite food for serving cold as an hors d'oeuvre with hot rice porridge, or congee. Since the Chinese palate leans toward savoriness, to contrast with the blandness of plain cooked rice (either the porridgy rice eaten at breakfast time or the drier steamed or boiled rice eaten at other meals), bean curd is usually tossed together with some strong-tasting ingredients (such as chopped pickle), or salty ingredients and spicy sauces when served as an hors d'oeuvre or in cold-tossed salads. For palates accustomed to vegetarian food, such hors d'oeuvres are appealing because of the subtle and satisfying flavor of "raw" bean curd and the sharp, tasty impact of the flavoring ingredients and sauces. Although the taste for such bean curd dishes is a cultivated one, it can quite easily be acquired, and once it is acquired the palate will always have a yearning for its combined simplicity and subtlety. Both the Chinese and the Japanese will go a long way to have an uncomplicated bean curd hors d'oeuvre or salad. These are usually served to start a meal, or during the meal as one of several dishes to complement the rice.

## COLD-TOSSED BEAN CURD WITH SESAME OR PEANUT BUTTER SAUCE

Serve with hot cooked rice or rice porridge (congee) along with two or more accompanying dishes.

*Serves 4, with rice*

3–4 cakes bean curd
2 tablespoons sesame paste or peanut butter
1 tablespoon vegetable oil
¾ tablespoon sesame oil

2½ tablespoons light soy sauce
1½ tablespoons cider vinegar

Drain the bean curd. Cut each cake into quarters and spread them on a serving dish. Mix the sesame paste or peanut butter with the vegetable oil and sesame oil until well blended. Mix the soy sauce with the vinegar. Place a large dollop of the sesame paste or peanut butter on top of each piece of bean curd and pour the soy sauce–vinegar mixture evenly over them.

## COLD-TOSSED BEAN CURD WITH CHINESE PICKLES

Serve with hot cooked rice or rice porridge (congee) along with two or more accompanying dishes.

Serves 4, with rice and other dishes

4 cakes bean curd
1½ tablespoons Sichuan Ja
   Tsai pickle (hot)
1½ tablespoons Tientsin snow
   pickle (salty and sour)

1½ tablespoons vegetable oil
1 tablespoon sesame oil
2½ tablespoons light soy
   sauce
1 tablespoon cider vinegar

Drain the bean curd and cut each cake into quarters. Chop the two pickles medium-fine and mix them together. Blend the oils together, and then the soy sauce and the vinegar.

Spread the bean curd pieces on a serving dish. Sprinkle an appropriate amount of chopped pickle and the soy sauce–vinegar mixture over each. Finally, drip a large drop or two of mixed oil over each piece of bean curd.

# HOT-TOSSED BEAN CURD
# IN SCALLION AND CORIANDER SAUCE

This dish will particularly appeal to anyone who likes the fragrance of coriander and the aroma of freshly chopped scallions.

Serves 4, with rice and other dishes

4 cakes bean curd
3 tablespoons vegetable oil
   (peanut or corn)
1 tablespoon finely chopped
   ginger root
1 tablespoon finely chopped
   Sichuan Ja Tsai pickle
3–4 tablespoons chopped fresh
   coriander leaves

3–4 tablespoons chopped scallions
2½ tablespoons light soy sauce
¾ tablespoon chili sauce
2 tablespoons vegetarian stock
1 tablespoon dry sherry
1½ teaspoons sugar

Cut each bean curd cake into quarters and poach in boiling water for 1 minute. Lift them out with a perforated spoon, drain, and place on a serving dish.

Heat the oil in a small frying pan or wok. When hot, add the ginger and pickle. Stir for 15–20 seconds. Add the chopped coriander leaves and scallions. Stir over medium heat for 1 minute. Add the soy sauce, chili sauce, stock, sherry, and sugar. Continue to stir all the ingredients together for a further ½ minute.

Pour the sauce and the ingredients in the frying pan or wok evenly over the bean curd in the serving dish and serve immediately.

# BEAN CURD WITH SPINACH AND RADISHES

The dark green of the spinach, the bright red and pink of the radish, and the whiteness of the bean curd make an attractive color contrast, and the flavor of each individual ingredient seems to stand out distinctly. Simple to prepare, this is an excellent dish to serve as an hors d'oeuvre.

Serves 4–6

2 cakes bean curd
8 ounces fresh red radishes
3 teaspoons salt
12 ounces young spinach

1½ teaspoons sugar
2 teaspoons light soy sauce
1½ tablespoons vegetable oil
½ tablespoon sesame oil

Drain the bean curd and cut into large sugar-lump-sized cubes. Rinse and trim the radishes. Give each radish a heavy bash with the side of a chopper, or a rolling pin. Sprinkle evenly with 2 teaspoons of the salt and leave to season for half an hour.

Poach the spinach in a large pan of boiling water for ½ minute. Drain thoroughly, and squeeze as dry as possible. Place on a chopping board and chop roughly. Place the chopped spinach in a large bowl. Add the remaining salt and the sugar, soy sauce, vegetable oil, and sesame oil. Turn and toss them together well and loosen them up. Add the bean curd cubes and toss them lightly with the spinach so that they are evenly mixed.

Spread the bean curd and spinach mixture evenly over a large serving dish. Drain the excess water from the seasoned radishes and dot them evenly over the bean curd and spinach.

# BEAN CURD SALAD WITH CHINESE SALT EGGS

This dish makes an excellent summer starter.

Serves 4 (or more with rice and other dishes)

2–3 cakes bean curd
1 romaine lettuce
3 medium tomatoes
1 bunch watercress
2 Chinese salt eggs (duck
  eggs, see page 53)
1½ tablespoons Sichuan Ja
  Tsai pickle

DRESSING:
2 tablespoons light soy sauce
1½ tablespoons cider or wine
  vinegar
1½ tablespoons vegetable oil
¾ tablespoon sesame oil

Cut the bean curd into large sugar-lump-sized pieces. Cut the lettuce into two or three pieces, and the tomatoes into eighths. Trim and roughly chop the watercress, chop the salt eggs, and finely mince the pickle.

Lay the lettuce leaves evenly over a serving dish. Spread the tomato sections and watercress over the lettuce. Spread the bean curd cubes on top of the vegetables. Mix the dressing ingredients together and drip the mixture over the bean curd and vegetables. Sprinkle the chopped pickle and salt eggs on top.

## BEAN CURD SALAD
## WITH BEAN SPROUTS
## AND HUNDRED-YEAR-OLD EGGS

Another excellent summer starter for any Chinese meal.

Serves 4 (or more with rice and other dishes)

Repeat the previous recipe, using ¼ pound bean sprouts instead of watercress, and adding 2 hundred-year-old eggs (see page 54). These eggs should be thoroughly washed (they are normally sold encrusted in mud), shelled, and cut into eight equal-sized segments. These segments should be placed evenly on top of the vegetable salad before it is sprinkled with the dressing, chopped salt eggs, and pickle.

## BEAN CURD WITH TOMATOES
## AND SCALLIONS

We Chinese are used to combining sweet-tasting ingredients with savory ones, especially for a starter or a side dish. Sliced tomatoes sprinkled with sugar are very frequently served in Peking in the summer.

Serves 4, with rice and other dishes

4–5 large, firm tomatoes
1½ tablespoons superfine
  granulated sugar
2–3 cakes bean curd
2½ tablespoons chopped scallions

DRESSING:
1½ tablespoons light soy
  sauce
1 tablespoon vegetable oil
½ tablespoon sesame oil

Slice the tomatoes, spread them in a single layer on a serving dish, and sprinkle with the sugar. Cut the bean curd into 8–12 cubes, place these on top of the tomatoes, and sprinkle with the chopped scallions. Mix together the ingredients for the dressing and pour evenly over the bean curd and tomatoes.

## CARROT AND CUCUMBER SALAD WITH BEAN CURD IN HOT SOY DRESSING

A good starter for a Chinese meal, in summer or winter.

Serves 4 (or more with rice and other dishes)

2 cakes bean curd
5–6 ounces young carrots
½ tablespoon salt
1 (six-inch) section of cucumber
HOT DRESSING:
2 chili peppers
2½ tablespoons vegetable oil

3 slices ginger root, shredded
2 tablespoons light soy sauce
3 tablespoons vegetarian stock
½ teaspoon salt
2 teaspoons chili sauce
1 tablespoon cider vinegar
¾ tablespoon sesame oil

Cut the bean curd into large sugar-lump-sized cubes. Rinse, trim, and scrape or peel the carrots, then cut them slantwise into ¼-inch diagonal sections. Parboil them for 5 minutes. Drain them thoroughly and sprinkle them with salt. Leave them to season for 1½ hours, and then drain away the extracted water and salt. Cut the cucumber (including the skin) into slightly larger diagonal sections. Trim and seed the chilies.

Heat the oil in a small frying pan or wok and fry the chilies and ginger over medium heat for 1¾ minutes. Add the soy sauce, stock, salt, and chili sauce. Stir-fry for ¾ minute. Remove from the heat and stir in the vinegar and sesame oil. Toss together the carrot, cucumber, and bean curd pieces in a bowl or deep-sided dish and pour the dressing evenly over them.

## COLD-TOSSED BEAN CURD WITH ONION, GINGER, AND SCALLION DRESSING

The strong flavors of cooked onion and fresh scallions make this dish remarkably appealing—if you like the taste of onion.

Serves 4 (or more with rice and other dishes)

3–4 cakes bean curd
1 small onion
3 slices ginger root
3 tablespoons vegetable oil
2 tablespoons light soy sauce
2 teaspoons red bean curd "cheese"
¼ teaspoon freshly ground black pepper

3 tablespoons vegetarian stock
1½ tablespoons dry sherry
1 tablespoon wine vinegar
3 tablespoons finely chopped scallion
2 teaspoons sesame oil

Cut each piece of bean curd into four pieces. Peel and coarsely chop the onion and finely chop the ginger.

Heat the oil in a small pan or wok. Add the onion and ginger and stir them in the hot oil for 1 minute over medium heat. Add the soy sauce, bean curd "cheese," pepper, stock, sherry, and vinegar. Continue to stir the ingredients together for 1 minute.

Spread the bean curd pieces on a serving dish. Pour a drip of the dressing on top of each piece of bean curd and place a large pinch of freshly chopped scallion on top. Sprinkle with sesame oil.

## COLD-TOSSED BEAN CURD WITH EGG, GARLIC-GINGER DRESSING, AND MIXED SAUCES

The contrast of flavor between the egg, dressing, and bean curd seems to bring out the subtle freshness of the bean curd.

Serves 4 (or more with rice and other dishes)

| | |
|---|---|
| 4 cakes bean curd | 1½ tablespoons hoisin sauce |
| 3 hard-boiled eggs | 2 teaspoons chili sauce |
| 2 cloves garlic | 1½ tablespoons vegetarian |
| 2 slices ginger root | stock |
| 1 teaspoon salt | 1 tablespoon dry sherry |
| ¾ teaspoon pepper | 1½ tablespoons vegetable oil |
| 2 tablespoons light soy sauce | ½ tablespoon sesame oil |

Cut each piece of bean curd into four pieces. Finely chop the eggs. Crush the garlic, finely chop with the ginger, and mash them in with the eggs, adding salt and pepper. Mix soy sauce, hoisin sauce, chili sauce, stock, sherry, and oils together to make the dressing.

Spread the bean curd on a serving dish. Add the seasoned egg mixture, toss together lightly, and sprinkle the dressing on top.

## COLD-TOSSED BEAN CURD WITH SOY EGG, SPINACH, AND MUSTARD DRESSING

Serves 4 (or more with rice and other dishes)

3 cakes bean curd
6 tablespoons dark soy sauce
3 hard-boiled eggs
8 ounces young spinach
1½ cloves garlic
2 slices ginger root
½ teaspoon salt
1½ tablespoons vegetable oil
1½ teaspoons sesame oil

DRESSING:
1 tablespoon dry mustard
2 tablespoons water
2 tablespoons light soy sauce
1 tablespoon wine vinegar
1 tablespoon dry sherry

Cut each piece of bean curd into eight pieces. Heat the soy sauce in a small saucepan, add the boiled eggs, and continue to heat slowly, turning the eggs over and over in the sauce until they are dark brown (about 4–5 minutes). Remove from the heat. When cool, cut each egg into six equal segments.

Poach the spinach in boiling water for 1 minute. Drain thoroughly, pile it up, and chop it into ½-inch pieces. Crush the garlic, and finely chop it together with the ginger. Mix the garlic, ginger, salt, and both the vegetable and sesame oils into the spinach. Turn and toss them together until well mixed.

Mix the dressing ingredients together until well blended. Spread the spinach on a serving dish. Place the soy egg segments and four bean curd pieces on top, well spaced out over the spinach, and sprinkle the dressing mixture evenly over them.

# COLD-TOSSED BEAN CURD WITH CHINESE PICKLES AND MARINADE

The contrast in flavor and texture between the pickles, the marinated ingredients, and the bean curd seems to bring out the fresh blandness of the latter.

*Serves 4 (or more with rice and other dishes)*

4 cakes bean curd
4–5 ounces canned Chinese marinated bamboo shoots
6 medium-sized Chinese dried black mushrooms
2 tablespoons dark soy sauce
1½ tablespoons dry sherry
2 tablespoons Sichuan Ja Tsai pickle, chopped

1½ tablespoons green snow pickle, chopped
1½ tablespoons Tientsin savory winter pickle, chopped
2 tablespoons light soy sauce
¾ tablespoon sesame oil

Cut each piece of bean curd into 8–10 cubes. Cut the bamboo shoots into slices approximately ½–¾ inch thick (if they are not already sliced). Soak the mushrooms in hot water for half an hour to soften. Drain. Remove and discard the stems and cut the caps into quarters. Soak them in the dark soy sauce and dry sherry for 30 minutes.

Place all the ingredients in a large bowl and toss them lightly together. Turn them out onto a serving dish and sprinkle with the light soy sauce and sesame oil.

# SOUPS

The quality of Chinese soups depends entirely on the quality of the stock used, and this is as true of Chinese vegetarian soups as of meat-based soups. Once the vegetarian stock is available (page 30), the eventual character of the soup is determined by adding briefly cooked ingredients to simmer for a short while in the stock. These ingredients may vary from leaf vegetables to root vegetables to vegetables such as tomato or cucumber that do not need much cooking; to pickles of all types; and to rehydrated dried vegetables, some of which are best added after a short period of stir-frying in a small amount of oil. This process, we Chinese believe, allows the flavor of the ingredients to be "exploded" by the heat into the oil and thereby more effectively communicated into the body of the soup.

Tofu soups have tofu, or bean curd, as one of their more substantial ingredients—usually added near the end, since tofu hardly needs cooking at all. Tofu is not added to contribute to the flavor of the soup, but more often as a contrast to the flavors and textures of the main ingredients. As such, it often has the effect of adding character as well as substance to the soup.

Tofu soups are often simply a follow-up to the making of ordinary vegetarian soups, so I shall include only a few recipes for them. Soy milk and soy mash can also be used to enrich soups. The mash is usually cooked along with the beans, cereals, and root vegetables in the preparation of the original stock, while the milk is added at a much later stage mainly to vary the flavor and increase the nutritiousness of the soup.

# CHINESE VEGETARIAN STOCK

Basic Chinese vegetarian stock is prepared by simmering together, for example, 2 pounds of mixed cereals: soybeans, sweet corn (cut into sections), soy mash, lentils, peanuts, and broad beans (or any three of these items) in 3½ to 4 quarts of water for 1½ hours, and then adding any three of the following items: potatoes, carrots, turnips, parsnips, broccoli stems, cauliflower stems, asparagus spears, and mushroom stems. Simmer together for a further 1½ hours. After 3 hours of slow simmering, the contents of the pot should be strained through a piece of cheesecloth placed in a sieve or colander. If the resulting broth is too strong or too thick, add water to dilute. These days many excellent vegetarian stock cubes are readily available, and a small amount may be added to strengthen or improve the flavor of the stock.

Once you have on hand a quantity of basic stock, the preparation of a wide variety of Chinese vegetarian soups becomes a quick and simple matter. At this stage dark-colored ingredients, such as soy sauce, should be added for seasoning if the soup is meant to be dark. This is often the case with tofu soups, since tofu is creamy white in color and bland and subtle in flavor. It is therefore well set off when contrasted with a dark and highly savory soup.

# HOT AND SOUR SOUP

This is a classic and popular Chinese soup. It is very satisfying, and especially good in winter, being hot, strong, and substantial.

Serves 4–5, with rice and other dishes

2–3 ounces bamboo shoots
2 slices ginger root

1 medium-sized onion
1 egg

2 vegetarian stock cubes
1 quart vegetarian stock
2 tablespoons dark soy sauce
2 cakes bean curd
6 medium-sized Chinese dried
  mushrooms
2 tablespoons vegetable oil
1 tablespoon chopped scallions
1 tablespoon chopped coriander leaves

2 teaspoons sesame oil
HOT AND SOUR SAUCE:
2 tablespoons light soy sauce
3 tablespoons wine vinegar
½ teaspoon freshly ground
  black pepper
2 tablespoons cornstarch dissolved in 5 tablespoons
  water

Cut the bamboo shoots into matchstick-sized strips. Cut the ginger into fine shreds. Cut the onion into thin slices. Beat the egg lightly in a bowl or cup. Dissolve the stock cubes in the stock and add the soy sauce. Cut the bean curd into sugar-lump-sized cubes. Soak the mushrooms in hot water for half an hour, drain, remove and discard the stems, and cut the caps into shreds.

Heat the vegetable oil in a saucepan. Add the ginger, onion, and mushrooms and stir over medium heat for 1½ minutes. Add the bamboo shoots and stir for 2 minutes. Pour in the stock, bring to a boil, and simmer for 5 minutes. Stir the hot and sour mixture until the ingredients are well blended and stir this into the soup, which should then thicken. When the soup starts to bubble again, beat the egg again and pour it in a thin stream along the prongs of a fork into the soup, trailing the stream evenly over the whole surface of the soup. The egg should set immediately, forming what we call in China an "egg-flower" effect. Now add the bean curd, which will increase the volume of the soup. Allow the soup to cook gently over medium heat for 3 more minutes.

The soup can be served in a large common soup bowl or tureen for people to help themselves from, or it can be divided into 4–5 individual soup bowls, and sprinkled with a pinch of chopped scallion and coriander, and sesame oil.

# MASHED BEAN CURD SOUP WITH CORN AND MUSHROOMS

This is another substantial and satisfying soup. Good to serve to add substance to a meal.

Serves 4–5, with rice and other dishes

6 medium-sized Chinese dried mushrooms
6 medium-sized firm button mushrooms
1 ounce Sichuan Ja Tsai pickle
1½ cakes bean curd
2 scallions
2 tablespoons vegetable oil

4 ounces canned corn kernels
1 quart vegetarian stock
1 vegetarian stock cube
1 tablespoon light soy sauce
3–4 tablespoons green peas
1½ tablespoons cornstarch dissolved in 4 tablespoons water
2 teaspoons sesame oil

Soak the dried mushrooms in hot water for half an hour and drain, reserving the mushroom water. Remove and discard the stems and roughly chop the caps. Cut each button mushroom vertically into quarters. Coarsely chop the pickle. Cut the bean curd into sugar-lump-sized cubes. Cut the scallions into ¼-inch pieces.

Heat the oil in a large saucepan. When hot, add both the dried and fresh mushrooms, the pickle, and the scallions. Stir over medium heat for 3 minutes. Pour in the mushroom water. Bring to a boil and simmer over low heat for 3 minutes. Add the canned corn and bean curd. Pour in the stock, in which the stock cube has been dissolved. Turn the heat up and bring contents to a boil. Reduce the heat and simmer for 5 minutes. Add the soy sauce and green peas. Stir them evenly into the soup. Stir the well-blended cornstarch mixture into the soup. Stir the soup and sprinkle in the sesame oil. Serve in the same manner as the previous soup.

# EGG-FLOWER AND SCALLION SOUP WITH BEAN CURD

Egg-flower soup has always been regarded as one of the simplest of Chinese soups. Because of the speed and ease with which it can be made, it is frequently seen on the family dining table. Since the soup is meant to be consumed with rice throughout most of the meal rather than eaten on its own, it should be served in a large soup bowl or tureen on the table so that diners can help themselves during the course of the meal.

Serves 4, with rice and other dishes

1 cake bean curd
1 egg
1 vegetarian stock cube
1 quart vegetarian stock
1½ tablespoons light soy
 sauce

1½ tablespoons coarsely
 chopped scallion
1½ tablespoons wine vinegar
salt and pepper to taste

Cut the bean curd into ¼-inch strips 2 inches long. Beat the egg lightly. Dissolve the stock cube in the stock and heat in a saucepan. When it boils, reduce heat to a simmer. Pour the beaten egg into the soup along the prongs of a fork in a very thin stream, trailing the stream evenly over the surface. Add the bean curd shreds. When the contents reboil, sprinkle with the soy sauce, chopped scallion, vinegar, and salt and pepper to taste.

## TURNIP AND TOMATO SOUP
## WITH BEAN CURD

This is a clear soup, containing a substantial quantity of vegetables, which can be regarded partly as a soup and partly as a savory dish to accompany rice.

Serves 4–5, with rice and other dishes

12 ounces turnips
1 cake bean curd
4–5 medium-sized tomatoes
3 cups water

1 vegetarian stock cube
1 tablespoon light soy sauce
1 quart vegetarian stock

Clean and cut the turnips into 1-inch wedges. Cut the bean curd into cubes roughly the same size, and each tomato into quarters or sixths.

Put the turnip wedges in a large saucepan with the water and bring to a boil. Add the stock cube and soy sauce, reduce the heat, and simmer gently for half an hour. Add the stock. When contents return to the boil, add the bean curd and tomato. Simmer for 5 more minutes and serve as in the previous recipe.

## BEAN CURD SOUP WITH SEAWEED,
## PEANUTS, MUSHROOMS, AND
## STEM AND HEART OF CABBAGE

As this soup should be entirely clear, only water is used in the cooking, rather than vegetarian stock, since the latter is often cloudy and it is a laborious process to remove all the cloudiness. This is a black and white soup, the mushroom, seaweed, and fungi being all black and the bean curd white. The stem of the cabbage, tenderized by the cooking, provides some large, distinctly vegetable-tasting pieces to bite into.

Serves 4–5, with rice and other dishes

1½ ounces hair seaweed (available from Chinese foodstores)

½–¾ ounce Chinese wood ears (tree fungi, available from Chinese foodstores)

6–8 medium-sized Chinese dried mushrooms

3 slices ginger root

1 ounce Sichuan Ja Tsai pickle

2 small young Chinese *bok choy* or savoy cabbage

2 cakes bean curd

2½ tablespoons vegetable oil

2 ounces roasted peanuts

6 cups water

1 vegetarian stock cube

1½ tablespoons light soy sauce

salt and pepper to taste

Soak the seaweed and fungi in hot water for 10 minutes and strain. Soak the dried mushrooms in 1 cup hot water for half an hour, then drain, reserving the water. Remove the stems and cut the caps into quarters. Cut the ginger and pickle into fine shreds. Remove all the outer leaves of the cabbage (for other uses), and the root ends of the stems. Cut the heart and stem of the cabbage into 1½–2-inch pieces. Cut the bean curd into 1-inch cubes.

Heat the oil in a large saucepan. When hot, add the mushrooms and peanuts and stir for 2 minutes. Add the ginger and pickle and continue to stir for 2 more minutes. Pour in the mushroom water and add the cabbage stem. When contents start to boil, reduce heat and simmer for 5 minutes. Add the heart of the cabbage, the fungi, and the seaweed and pour in the water. Bring to a boil, reduce the heat, and simmer for half an hour. Add the bean curd, stock cube, and soy sauce, and adjust for seasoning with salt and pepper.

# SOYBEANS, BEAN SPROUTS, AND BEAN CURD SOUP

This substantial soup can be consumed throughout the meal as an additional dish.

*Serves 5–6, with rice and other dishes*

8 ounces dried soybeans
1 pound fresh bean sprouts
2 cakes bean curd
3½–4 tablespoons vegetable
  oil
1 quart water

2 cups vegetarian stock
1 vegetarian stock cube
1 teaspoon salt
1 teaspoon sugar
1 tablespoon light soy sauce
1 teaspoon sesame oil

Soak soybeans in water overnight. Drain well. Rinse bean sprouts well to clean them of their roots, or as many of them as possible. Set sprouts aside. Cut the bean curd into large sugar-lump-sized cubes.

Heat the oil in a saucepan. When hot, add the beans and stir-fry over medium heat for 4–5 minutes. Add the sprouts and continue to stir-fry for 3–4 minutes. Add the water and bring to a boil. Reduce the heat and simmer gently for 1 hour.

Add the bean curd, stock and crumbled stock cube, salt, sugar, and soy sauce. Bring back to a boil and then simmer gently for 2 minutes. Sprinkle the soup with sesame oil and serve.

## SPINACH AND BEAN CURD SOUP

Serves 4–5, with rice and other dishes

8 ounces fresh spinach
2 cloves garlic
3½ tablespoons vegetable oil
1 teaspoon salt
2 cups water
2 cups vegetarian stock
1 vegetarian stock cube

1 tablespoon soy sauce
1 cake bean curd
1½ tablespoons cornstarch
 blended in 4 tablespoons
 water
1 teaspoon sesame oil

Wash the spinach and drain it well. Pile it up and slice it at 1-inch intervals. Coarsely crush the garlic. Cut the bean curd into large sugar-lump-sized cubes.

Heat the oil in a large, deep wok. When hot, add the spinach and salt and turn in the oil until the spinach has softened. Add the water and bring to a boil. Add the vegetarian stock, stock cube, and soy sauce. Bring back to a boil, add the bean curd pieces, then lower the heat and cook gently for 4–5 minutes, turning the contents over a few times so as to mix the ingredients more evenly. Sprinkle in the blended cornstarch and the sesame oil. Give the contents one more turn and serve in the same manner as in the previous recipe.

## BEAN CURD SOUP WITH FAVA BEANS AND CHINESE SNOW PICKLE

Like most bean curd soups this is a substantial soup. It can be served either as a soup or as a main course dish, along with other dishes served during the course of the meal.

Serves 4–5, with rice and other dishes

| | |
|---|---|
| 8 ounces fava beans | 2 cups vegetarian stock |
| 1–2 red chilies | 1 vegetarian stock cube |
| 2–3 ounces snow pickle | 2 tablespoons light soy sauce |
| 1½ cakes bean curd | 1 teaspoon sugar |
| 2 tablespoons vegetable oil | pepper to taste |
| 2 cups water | 1 tablespoon sesame oil |

Soak the beans overnight, or until the seed coats can be easily removed. Rinse the beans under running water. Place them in a saucepan, add fresh water, and boil for 30 minutes. Drain the beans and mash them into a purée.

Trim and seed the chilies and coarsely chop them and the snow pickle. Cut the bean curd into sugar-lump-sized pieces.

Heat the oil in a saucepan. When hot, add the pickle and chilies and stir-fry for 2 minutes. Add the water and bring to a boil. Add the bean purée and the vegetarian stock and stock cube. When contents reboil, reduce heat to low, add the bean curd, and simmer for 5–6 minutes, stirring gently all the time. Add soy sauce, sugar, and pepper to taste. Sprinkle with the sesame oil and serve.

# STIR-FRIED BEAN CURD DISHES

There are two types of stir-fried bean curd dishes. Either they contain pressed bean curd, which is cut into strips or thin slices and stir-fried with a variety of vegetables, similarly cut into strips or sliced; or mashed bean curd, which is stir-fried with strong-flavored ingredients and sauces. This latter type is usually served as a topping on plain boiled rice or noodles, while the former is usually served as one of several dishes accompanied by rice or other bulk foods, such as noodles, steamed buns, soft rice (or rice porridge), or vegetable fried rice.

## PRESSED BEAN CURD

Pressed bean curd is made by extracting more water from the bean curd. This can be done when the bean curd is still being made, at the stage when the freshly formed curd is wrapped and covered with cheesecloth and a weight is placed on top of it to press it into shape (page 17). Now, if the weight placed on top of the curd is increased by three or four times (to 8–10 pounds), and the time during which the curd is being pressed is lengthened to over eight hours or overnight, the water in the curd should have drained out slowly and much more thoroughly. The resultant substance should be much drier and firmer in texture than usual. In China this firmer and drier form of bean curd is simply called dried bean curd, or *toufukan*.

Processing the pressed bean curd is not complete until it has been submerged in a marinade consisting of 4–5 tablespoons of soy sauce added to 2 cups of water together with 1 tablespoon sugar, 2 teaspoons salt, and 3–4 pieces of star anise. The mixture is brought very slowly and gently to the boil, and the bean curd is allowed to simmer in the marinade for a further 7–8 minutes. It should then be removed from the heat and allowed to rest overnight, after which it should be drained and cut into strips, slices, or cubes (or any other appropriate shape or size).

Pressed bean curd can also be produced from ready-made bean curd, or tofu, simply by laying the bean curd pieces out in a single layer, covering them with cheesecloth, and subjecting them overnight to 6–8 pounds of pressure applied by a flat weight on top of the bean curd. The much firmer and drier form of bean curd is then cooked in the same marinade as described above, and left submerged in it overnight. When the pressed bean curd is drained, it is ready to be cut into sizes appropriate for whatever culinary purpose.

༄

## STIR-FRY OF SHREDDED PRESSED BEAN CURD WITH THREE SHREDDED INGREDIENTS

This dish is popular in the Lower Yangtze area. It is served on the table, along with other dishes, for consuming with rice.

*Serves 4–5, with rice and other dishes*

4–5 ounces pressed bean curd
2–3 young carrots
2–3 ounces snow peas
4–5 slices ginger root
3 tablespoons vegetable oil
4 tablespoons vegetarian stock

SAUCE:
1½ tablespoons soy sauce
½ tablespoon yellow bean
  sauce (paste)
1 tablespoon hoisin sauce
1½ tablespoons dry sherry
1 teaspoon sugar
1 tablespoon sesame oil

Cut the pressed bean curd into 1½-inch matchstick-sized strips. Scrape or peel the carrots, trim the snow peas, and cut them both into similar-sized strips. Cut the ginger into fine shreds.

Heat the vegetable oil in a frying pan or wok. When hot, add the ginger and stir for half a minute, followed by the carrots and snow peas. Stir and turn them over medium heat for 2 minutes. Finally, add the pressed bean curd strips and the vegetarian stock. Continue to stir and turn them together for 3 more minutes, or until nearly all the liquid has evaporated.

Now add all the sauce ingredients and mix them together with all the shredded vegetables in the pan. Continue to stir and turn for about 2–2½ minutes, or until the pressed bean curd and the vegetables are evenly coated with the sauce.

## HOT-TOSSED PRESSED BEAN CURD WITH CELERY AND SICHUAN JA TSAI PICKLE

This is quite a spicy dish, and is suitable to serve and eat with quantities of plain boiled rice.

Serves 4–5, with rice and other dishes

4 ounces pressed bean curd
4–6 ounces celery
1½–2 ounces Sichuan Ja Tsai
  pickle
3 slices ginger root
2 scallions
3½–4 tablespoons vegetable
  oil

SAUCE OR DRESSING:
1½ tablespoons soy sauce
½ teaspoon sugar
5 tablespoons vegetarian stock
½ vegetarian stock cube
2 teaspoons chili sauce

Cut the pressed bean curd and celery into ¼-inch strips 2 inches long, the pickle and ginger into fine shreds, and the scallions into 2-inch sections.

Heat the oil in a frying pan or wok. When hot, add the ginger and pickle. Stir for half a minute. Add the celery, pressed bean curd, and scallions. Continue to stir and turn over medium heat for 2½ minutes. Add all the sauce ingredients and continue to stir and turn over high heat for another 2 minutes.

# HOT-TOSSED PRESSED BEAN CURD WITH SHREDDED FRESH BEAN CURD, MUSHROOMS, AND CELERY

This is a highly savory dish. Two fresh ingredients (bean curd and mushrooms) and two seasoned ingredients (marinated, pressed bean curd and dried mushrooms) are tossed and stir-fried together in flavored oil. The shredded celery provides a contrast in texture. Serve with other dishes and quantities of plain boiled rice.

Serves 5–6, with rice and other dishes

1 cake bean curd
3 ounces pressed bean curd
6 medium-sized Chinese dried
  mushrooms
8 ounces large button
  mushrooms
2 scallions
3 slices ginger root
2 cloves garlic
4 tablespoons vegetable oil
¾ teaspoon salt

1 stalk celery
5 tablespoons vegetarian stock
SAUCE:
1½ tablespoons light soy
  sauce
1 tablespoon hoisin sauce
2 teaspoons chili sauce
1½ tablespoons dry sherry
1 teaspoon sugar
1 tablespoon tomato paste

Cut both bean curds into ¼-inch strips 2 inches long. Soak the dried mushrooms for half an hour in hot water. Drain. Discard the stems and cut the caps and the fresh mushrooms into strips similar to the bean curd. Cut the scallions into ¼-inch pieces, separating the white parts from the green. Shred the ginger, and coarsely crush and chop the garlic. Shred the celery.

Heat the oil in a frying pan or wok. When hot, add the ginger, garlic, white parts of the scallions, dried mushrooms, and pressed bean curd. Stir-fry for 3 minutes over medium heat. Add the fresh mushrooms, salt, celery, and stock, and continue to stir-fry for 3 more minutes. Add the fresh bean curd and all the sauce ingredients. Turn and stir all the ingredients together for 1½ minutes, until they are all evenly mixed and well coated.

## DEEP-FRIED BEAN CURD STIR-FRIED WITH MUSHROOMS AND BROCCOLI

This is another rice-accompanying dish often seen on Chinese tables. The bean curd provides the meatlike protein, the mushrooms add savoriness, and the lightly cooked broccoli contributes the crisp taste of fresh vegetables.

Serves 4–5, with rice and other dishes

1½ cakes bean curd
vegetable oil for deep-frying
6–8 medium-sized Chinese
　dried mushrooms
1 medium-sized onion
8 ounces broccoli
3 tablespoons vegetable oil
3 slices ginger root

4 tablespoons vegetarian stock
SAUCE:
2 tablespoons light soy sauce
1 tablespoon hoisin sauce
2 teaspoons chili sauce
1½ tablespoons dry sherry
1 teaspoon sugar

Cut the bean curd into 1-by-1½-inch flat pieces. Deep-fry them in hot oil for 2–2½ minutes, until the surfaces are somewhat firm and yellow. Drain thoroughly. Soak the mushrooms in boiling water for half an hour. Drain. Discard the stems and cut the caps into halves. Cut the onion into thin slices. Break the broccoli into individual florets and cut the stem into 1-inch wedges.

Heat the vegetable oil in a large frying pan or wok. When hot, add the onion, ginger, broccoli stems, and mushrooms and stir-fry in the hot oil for 2 minutes, to season the oil. Add the broccoli and stock and continue to stir-fry for 1½ minutes, and then cook, covered, for 1½ minutes. Uncover the pan or wok, pour the sauce ingredients over the contents, and continue to turn and stir-fry all ingredients together for a further 1½ minutes.

# VEGETARIAN MU SHOU ROU, OR SHREDDED BEAN CURD WITH GOLDEN NEEDLES, MUSHROOMS, WOOD EARS, AND EGGS

This is a favorite dish of North China. Its vegetarian version is popular throughout the country.

Serves 4–5, with rice and other dishes

1 cake bean curd
vegetable oil for deep-frying
2 ounces wood ears
2 ounces golden needles (tiger
  lily buds, available at
  Chinese foodstores)
4–5 medium-sized Chinese
  dried mushrooms
2 scallions
2 cloves garlic
3 tablespoons vegetable oil

½ teaspoon salt
3 eggs
1 teaspoon sesame oil
SAUCE:
1½ tablespoons light soy
  sauce
1 tablespoon yellow bean
  sauce (paste)
1 tablespoon dry sherry
1 teaspoon sugar
2 tablespoons vegetarian stock

Cut the bean curd into ¼-inch strips 2 inches long. Deep-fry for 1½ minutes and drain thoroughly. Soak the wood ears and golden needles in water for 4–5 minutes, rinse, and drain. Soak the mushrooms in hot water for half an hour and drain. Remove and discard the stems. Cut each cap into quarters. Cut the scallions into ¼-inch pieces, separating the white parts from the green. Crush and chop the garlic.

Heat half the vegetable oil in a frying pan or wok. When hot, add the white parts of the scallions, the mushrooms, and the garlic. Stir-fry for 1½ minutes. Add the salt, bean curd, wood ears, and golden needles. Stir-fry for 1½ minutes over medium heat and then put aside.

Heat the remaining oil in another pan or wok. Beat the eggs lightly and pour them in. When about to set, add half the green parts of the scallions, stir and break the egg up into 1–1½-inch pieces, and remove from the heat.

Place the original pan or wok over medium heat. When the ingredients start to sizzle, pour in all the sauce ingredients and turn and stir them around quickly until all the other ingredients are well coated. Add the eggs to the same pan or wok and turn and toss everything together. Sprinkle with the remainder of the scallions and the seasame oil and serve.

## STIR-FRIED BEAN CURD WITH GREEN BEANS IN HOT SAUCE

This is a spicy dish, suitable for consuming with quantities of plain boiled rice.

*Serves 4–5, with rice and other dishes*

12 ounces green beans
1½ cakes bean curd
3 cloves garlic
3½ tablespoons vegetable oil
½ teaspoon salt

SAUCE:
1 tablespoon light soy sauce
1 tablespoon hoisin sauce
½ tablespoon yellow bean
   sauce (paste)

2 teaspoons chili sauce
2 teaspoons oil (Chinese chili
   oil—optional)

1 tablespoon tomato
   paste

Trim the green beans and cut each one in half. Boil them in ample water for 2 minutes and drain well. Cut the bean curd into ¾-inch cubes. Crush and chop the garlic.

Heat the oil in a frying pan or wok. When hot, add the garlic, salt, and green beans. Stir-fry over medium heat for 2½ minutes. Add the bean curd pieces and turn them lightly with the beans for 1½ minutes. Pour in all the sauce ingredients. Turn and stir them together for 1 minute. Cook and turn for 1½ more minutes and serve.

## HOT-TOSSED DICED PRESSED BEAN CURD WITH GREEN PEAS, BAMBOO SHOOTS, DRIED MUSHROOMS, STRAW MUSHROOMS, AND ZUCCHINI OR EGGPLANT

Another somewhat spicy dish, excellent with plain boiled rice.

Serves 5–6, with other dishes

8 ounces pressed bean curd
3–4 ounces bamboo shoots
1 medium-sized zucchini or 1
   small eggplant
4–5 medium-sized Chinese
   dried mushrooms
1 medium-sized onion
2 cloves garlic
1 green and 1 red chili

3 tablespoons vegetable oil
½ teaspoon salt
1 tablespoon Chinese winter
   pickle (Dung Tsai)
1 small can straw mushrooms
3 ounces green peas (fresh or
   frozen)
2 teaspoons sesame oil

SAUCE:
1½ tablespoons light soy
   sauce
2 teaspoons red bean curd
   "cheese"

1½ tablespoons dry sherry
6 tablespoons vegetarian stock
1 teaspoon sugar
1½ teaspoons chili sauce

Cut the pressed bean curd into cubes the size of half a sugar lump. Cut the bamboo shoots and zucchini or eggplant into similar-sized cubes (leaving on the skin). Soak the dried mushrooms in hot water for half an hour, drain, discard the stems, and cut the caps into quarters. Cut the onion into very thin slices, crush and chop the garlic, trim and seed the chilies and cut them into thin shreds.

Heat the oil in a frying pan or wok. When hot, add the onion, garlic, and chilies and stir-fry for half a minute over medium heat. Add the salt, pressed bean curd, dried mushrooms, and pickle, and stir-fry them all together over high heat for 1½ minutes. Add the bamboo shoots, straw mushrooms, peas, zucchini or eggplant, and continue to stir-fry for a further 1½ minutes. Add the sauce ingredients and turn and stir the contents of the wok or frying pan vigorously. Cover the pan, reduce the heat to medium-low, and cook gently for 5 minutes. Remove the lid, sprinkle contents with sesame oil, and serve.

## STEAMED STUFFED CUCUMBER CUPS WITH MASHED BEAN CURD AND CHOPPED PRESSED BEAN CURD

These cucumber cups, covered with a reddish-brown sauce, make a picturesque dish and a useful starter for a Chinese vegetarian meal.

Serves 4–6, with other dishes

2 large cucumbers
2 ounces pressed bean curd
1 cake bean curd
4 medium-sized dried mush-
　rooms
1 clove garlic
2 slices ginger root
2 scallions
3 tablespoons vegetable oil
½ teaspoon salt

SAUCE:
1½ tablespoons light soy
　sauce
1½ teaspoons red bean curd
　"cheese"
1 tablespoon hoisin sauce
½ tablespoon Sichuan chili-
　soy paste
2 tablespoons vegetarian stock
1 tablespoon chili sauce
1 tablespoon vegetable oil

Peel the cucumbers and cut them into 2½-inch sections. Scoop out the insides to a depth of 2 inches, making cucumber cups with ½ inch left at the bottom of each cup. Chop the pressed bean curd coarsely. Mash the bean curd cake. Soak the dried mushrooms in hot water for half an hour. Drain. Discard the stems and coarsely chop the caps. Finely chop the garlic and ginger. Cut the scallions into ¼-inch shavings (keeping the white separate from the greens).

Heat the oil in a frying pan or wok. When hot, add the ginger and garlic, the white part of the scallions, the salt, and the chopped pressed bean curd and stir-fry over medium heat for 2 minutes. Add the mashed bean curd and continue to stir-fry for a further 2 minutes.

Stuff the stir-fried ingredients into the cucumber cups until each cup is filled to the brim. Arrange the cups, well spaced out, in a flat, heatproof dish. Insert the dish into a steamer and steam vigorously for 5–6 minutes.

While the cucumber cups are steaming, heat and stir the sauce ingredients together in a small saucepan until they are well blended and beginning to boil.

Remove the dish from the steamer and drain away any water that may have collected during the steaming. Pour the sauce from the small saucepan over the contents of the cucumber cups and serve.

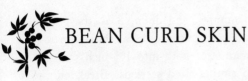

# BEAN CURD SKIN

This is the skin of bean curd milk, and is usually available dried in stick form, 6–9 inches long. It is firm and crispy in texture and requires softening by soaking in hot water or cooking in stock. In Chinese cooking it is mostly used in braised "semi-soup" dishes, which occur frequently on the Chinese table as a contrast to stir-fried dishes. It is also sometimes included in stir-fried dishes, especially those containing hard vegetables, where the ingredients need to be cooked or braised for a somewhat longer time than is normally required in stir-frying.

## BRAISED BEAN CURD SKIN WITH TRANSPARENT NOODLES (OR BEAN-STARCH THREADS)

This is a useful semi-soup dish for serving at an informal meal as an alternative to stir-fried dishes.

*Serves 5–6, with other dishes*

3 sticks bean curd skin
1 ounce golden needles
3–4 ounces transparent
  noodles
4–5 ounces broccoli
3 medium-sized slices Sichuan
  Ja Tsai pickle

2 slices ginger root
3 tablespoons vegetable oil
½ teaspoon salt
1½ cups vegetarian stock
3–4 ounces bean sprouts
2 tablespoons light soy sauce

Break the bean curd skin sticks into quarters, add to a large saucepan of warm water, and slowly bring to the boil. Turn off the heat, leave to soak for a further 30–40 minutes, and drain. Soak the golden needles in hot water for 5 minutes and drain. Also soak the transparent noodles for 5 minutes and drain. Cut both into 1½-inch sections, and the bean curd skin into similar-sized sections. Break off the broccoli florets and cut them into 1½-inch pieces. Shred the pickle and ginger.

Heat the oil in a frying pan. When hot, add the pickle and ginger followed by the salt, bean curd skin, and broccoli. Stir them together with the other ingredients for 2½ minutes. Pour in the stock. When it boils, add the bean sprouts and noodles. Allow the contents to simmer for 8 minutes, then add soy sauce.

## SAUTÉED BEAN CURD SKIN IN MUSHROOM OIL WITH ASPARAGUS AND FRESH MUSHROOMS

This is a very tasty combination of foods that can be served with the majority of other dishes and consumed with rice. The enjoyment of the chewiness of the bean curd skin together with crunchy or soft vegetables is a cultivated taste that we Chinese appreciate a lot.

Serves 5–6, with other dishes

MUSHROOM OIL:
6–8 medium-sized dried
  mushrooms
1 pound fresh mushrooms
6 tablespoons vegetable oil
1½ tablespoons light soy
  sauce

4–5 sticks bean curd skin
1 pound fresh asparagus
8 ounces fresh button
  mushrooms
2 tablespoons vegetable oil
½ teaspoon salt
5–6 tablespoons vegetarian
  stock

1½ tablespoons light soy
   sauce
2 teaspoons bean curd
   "cheese" (white or red)

4–5 tablespoons mushroom
oil with sautéed
mushrooms (prepared as
described below)

First prepare the mushroom oil. Soak the dried mushrooms in hot water for 30 minutes, then drain. Discard the stems and cut the caps into shreds. Clean and cut the fresh mushrooms vertically through the stems into quarters or sixths.

Heat the 6 tablespoons of oil in a saucepan or wok. When hot, add the dried mushrooms and stir-fry for 1½ minutes. Add the fresh mushrooms and stir-fry for 3 minutes over medium heat. Add the soy sauce, reduce the heat to low, and continue to stir-fry for 2 minutes. Leave contents to simmer gently and sauté for a further 8 minutes, stirring and turning occasionally. When all the moisture has evaporated, the mushroom substance and oil should be very flavorful. They can be used independently by straining the oil from the mushrooms, or simply by using spoonfuls of the oil and the fried mushrooms together.

Break each stick of bean curd skin into quarters. Add to a large pan of water and bring slowly to a boil. Leave to soak for 30 minutes, then drain, and cut into 1½-inch sections. Rinse the asparagus, trim off the hard white bottoms, and cut into 2½–3-inch sections, separating the tips from the rest of the spears. Clean the button mushrooms and cut them vertically into quarters.

Heat the 2 tablespoons of oil in a saucepan or wok. When hot, add the asparagus except for the tips, the bean curd skin, and salt, and stir-fry for 2 minutes. Add the vegetarian stock and sauté over low heat for 4–5 minutes. Now add the asparagus tips, fresh mushrooms, soy sauce, bean curd "cheese," mushroom oil, and sautéed mushrooms. Stir and mix all the ingredients together for 2½ minutes over medium heat. Reduce the heat to low and allow contents to simmer-sauté together for 2½ minutes.

## SAUTÉED BEAN CURD SKIN IN
## MUSHROOM OIL WITH BABY CORN
## AND BROCCOLI

Since mushroom oil and sautéed mushrooms (see above) are so flavorful, they can naturally be used to cook with other combinations
of ingredients, in this case with baby corn and broccoli. This dish
provides a colorful mixture of vegetables and goes well with Chinese
noodles or plain boiled rice.

Serves 5–6, with other dishes

12 ounces broccoli
6–8 ounces canned baby corn
3–4 sticks bean curd skin
3 tablespoons vegetable oil
1½ tablespoons light soy
    sauce

4 tablespoons vegetarian stock
5–6 tablespoons mushroom
    oil with sautéed
    mushrooms
2 teaspoons sesame oil

Break the broccoli into individual florets. Cut the stems into 1½-
inch wedges. Drain the baby corn. Prepare the bean curd skin as in
the previous recipe.

Heat the oil in a frying pan or wok. When hot, add the broccoli
wedges and bean curd skin and stir-fry them over medium heat for
2 minutes. Add the soy sauce, stock, baby corn, and broccoli florets.
Turn and stir them together for 1 minute and leave them to sauté
together for 2½ minutes, or until most of the moisture has evaporated.
Add the mushroom oil and sautéed mushrooms and stir with the
other ingredients for 1 minute. Leave all the ingredients to sauté
together over low heat for 3 minutes. Sprinkle with sesame oil. Stir,
turn once more, and serve.

# 2 EGGS

Eggs usually come in four main forms or styles: marbled tea eggs, soy eggs, salt eggs, and "hundred-year-old eggs."

*Marbled tea eggs* are hard-boiled eggs that have had their shells slightly cracked, are reboiled in strong tea, and left to soak in the latter for a period of time. The process not only allows the tea flavor to penetrate, but also enables the small amount of tea that seeps through the cracked shells to form a marbled pattern on the white surface of the boiled eggs.

*Soy eggs* are hard-boiled eggs, with their shells removed, that are cooked for a short while in soy sauce. This cooking and soaking rapidly causes the eggs to turn the dark brown of the soy sauce. The soy sauce coating not only helps the eggs to keep longer, but its rich salty flavor and the contrast with the egg white underneath also seems to make them more appealing to eat with rice, especially with rice porridge, or congee, which is standard food for a Chinese breakfast. Soy eggs are one of the most frequently seen items on the Chinese breakfast table, and are often eaten while traveling and at picnics.

*Salt eggs* are usually duck or goose eggs that have been boiled and steeped in brine. This process causes the yolk to turn orangey red. Because of the saltiness of such eggs, they are also a favorite item on the Chinese breakfast table, where bland rice porridge, or congee, is consumed and the majority of accompaniments served have to be pickled or salty to provide a contrast.

*Hundred-year-old eggs.* This is of course a nickname. It would probably be more accurate to call "hundred-year-old-eggs" "pickled eggs," since they are lengthily "pickled" in a mixture of mud and lime. When bought—unlike the other types of eggs, they are hardly ever made at home—not only are they encrusted with thick mud but also a layer of chopped straw. This helps to keep the eggs apart while they are stored together in a large earthen jar to mature for several months. During this period, the eggs have to be turned around a number of times. The eggs (usually duck eggs) are in fact very slowly "cooked" by the heat generated when water is added to the mud-and-lime mixture. After the necessary period of "incubating," the egg white will have turned dark green and the yolk orangey green. Between them they emit a sulphurous odor which presages an eggy savoriness that is highly appealing to the cultivated and converted. Apart from being eaten for breakfast, these eggs are also often cut into wedges and served as hors d'oeuvres at a multi-course party dinner; alternatively they are steamed together in a savory egg custard along with tea eggs, salt eggs, or quail eggs in a multi-egg dish, where the three or four different types and colors of egg are presented together, all partly immersed in the yellow custard. Quail eggs are not considered serious food in China because of their small size, but they are useful for decorative purposes in an array of items for a large party dish.

As already indicated, these four types of eggs can be eaten on their own or with one another; or they can be cut into slices, wedges, or smaller pieces and further cooked by steaming or stir-frying with other foods to create a large number of other dishes to which these "seasoned" eggs can contribute their own inimitable flavor.

An ordinary beaten egg is of course even more versatile than seasoned eggs. Apart from being extremely quick and convenient to cook, it can easily be combined with most vegetables by stir-frying them together; or if the vegetables are easily tenderized, they can be steamed together in an egg custard. Because the method of steaming is prevalent in Chinese kitchens and steamed savory egg custard is eminently suitable and appealing to eat with rice, it is an extremely popular dish in Chinese home cooking.

But it is in stir-frying that eggs produce by far the largest number of dishes, and they can in most cases be prepared and produced in a very short time. Chinese stir-fried egg dishes are something in between a Western scrambled egg and an omelet—the beaten eggs cooking in a pan are usually stirred just before they set. If other ingredients are incorporated and cooked together with them, the result is usually somewhat flat, like a Spanish omelet or an Italian *frittata*. Like Western omelets, Chinese stir-fried egg dishes incorporate other ingredients and food materials to improve or vary the flavor or color of the dish. To achieve this variety in our vegetarian cooking, we often start by using chopped pickles or garlic to season and flavor the oil used, and at the end the egg dish is sprinkled with a small amount of finely and freshly chopped aromatic ingredients, such as chopped chives, scallions, coriander leaves, or flower petals, sometimes with the addition of wine and soy sauce. In between, larger quantities of quick-to-cook colorful vegetables, such as tomato, red or green peppers, spinach, bean sprouts, mushrooms, broccoli florets, or asparagus tips, may be incorporated, some of which need to be stir-fried separately and only thrown together with the beaten egg in the last moment's final assembly, when the egg has still not quite set.

In such cooking, timing is of the essence, and great dishes can be created out of ordinary materials. But to ease the demand made on the skill of the cook, equally appealing dishes can be produced by cooking the vegetables quite independently of the "scrambled omelet." These can be arranged in a bed on a serving dish with the egg placed on top. Just a word on the effect of wine and soy sauce on Chinese scrambled omelets: a small amount of hot wine (Chinese rice wine is usually heated before drinking), and an even smaller amount of good quality soy sauce (1 to 2 tablespoons) poured over the omelet just before serving, are quite capable of lifting what amounts to an ordinary household dish to something altogether finer. Note that the combined use of chopped scallions *(chung hua)* and soy sauce is a must when serving stir-fried eggs, as they seem to have the effect of emphasizing the egginess as well as increasing the aromatic appeal.

# STIR-FRIED EGG DISHES

## SIMPLE STIR-FRIED EGGS

Although there are many other dishes which can be eaten with rice, these stir-fried eggs have a unique appeal.

Serves 4–6, with other dishes

5–6 eggs
4–5 tablespoons vegetable oil
2½ tablespoons chopped
  scallions or chives

¼ teaspoon freshly ground
  pepper
1½ tablespoons good quality
  soy sauce

Beat the eggs lightly with a fork or a pair of chopsticks for 10–15 seconds, or until blended.

Heat the oil in a frying pan or wok. When hot, reduce the heat to low. Pour in the beaten egg, making sure it spreads evenly over the pan. Sprinkle the egg with half the scallions or chives and the pepper. Allow the egg to cook gently for about 1½–1¾ minutes, when it should be about three-quarters set. Turn and stir the eggs, then transfer them to a well-heated serving dish with a spatula or perforated spoon (thus straining away any excess oil). When the eggs are still quite hot, sprinkle them with the remaining scallions or chives and the soy sauce.

## STIR-FRIED EGGS WITH SPINACH

This is a simple but attractive dish, and is extremely appealing with plain boiled rice.

Serves 6–8, with other dishes

12 ounces young spinach
3–4 cloves garlic
4 tablespoons vegetable oil
1 teaspoon salt

1½ teaspoons sesame oil
stir-fried egg mixture (see above)

Trim and rinse the spinach well and dry thoroughly. Crush and coarsely chop the garlic.

Heat the oil in a frying pan or wok. When hot, add the garlic and stir-fry over medium heat for 15 seconds. Add the salt and then the spinach, and spread evenly over the pan. After 30–45 seconds turn and stir-fry it over high heat for 1–1½ minutes. By this time the spinach should be well glossed and lubricated by the hot oil.

Transfer the spinach to a well-heated serving dish, spreading it out evenly, sprinkle with sesame oil, and place the stir-fried egg on top.

## STIR-FRIED EGGS WITH SOYBEAN MASH, PEAS, AND STRAW MUSHROOMS

This is a fairly substantial dish, and should add bulk and nutrition to a family meal.

Serves 5–6, with other dishes

3–4 eggs
1 teaspoon salt
5 tablespoons vegetable oil
2 cloves garlic, chopped
2 tablespoons snow pickle,
    coarsely chopped
3–4 tablespoons green peas,
    fresh or frozen

4–5 tablespoons straw
    mushrooms, or firm
    button mushrooms
    chopped to the same size as
    straw mushrooms
4–5 ounces mashed bean curd
    (see page 38)
1½ tablespoons chopped
    scallions

Lightly beat the eggs with ½ teaspoon salt for ten seconds. Heat 3 tablespoons of the oil in a frying pan or wok. When hot, add the garlic and pickle and stir-fry for half a minute. Add the peas, mushrooms, and soybean mash and stir-fry over high heat for 2 minutes, then push them to one side of the pan. Add the remaining 2 tablespoons of oil to the other side, and when this is hot, pour in the beaten egg. After 1 minute, and when the eggs have set, scramble them, and then scramble the other ingredients in the pan together with the eggs. Reduce the heat to low and sprinkle contents with the chopped scallion and the remaining salt. Continue to stir-fry all the ingredients together for 1–1½ more minutes and serve.

## STIR-FRIED EGGS WITH TOMATOES

Serves 4–5, with other dishes

4–5 eggs
5 firm, medium-sized
    tomatoes

4½ tablespoons vegetable oil
2 scallions, chopped (separate
    white from greens)

1–2 slices ginger root,
  chopped fine
1¼ teaspoons salt
1½ teaspoons sugar

1 tablespoon soy sauce
1 tablespoon dry sherry
pepper to taste

Beat the eggs lightly with a fork or chopsticks for 10–15 seconds until blended. Cut each tomato into quarters.

Heat 2½ tablespoons of the vegetable oil in a frying pan or wok. When hot, add the whites of the scallions and the ginger. Stir them in the hot oil for half a minute. Add the tomatoes and sprinkle with salt and sugar. Turn and stir-fry for 1 minute, then push contents to one side of the pan. Add the remaining oil to the other side. When hot, pour in the beaten eggs. After 1 minute, turn and stir-fry the eggs lightly for half a minute. Bring the tomatoes over to mix and stir-fry together with the eggs. Sprinkle with soy sauce, scallion greens, sherry, and pepper. Turn and stir the contents together once more and transfer to a well-heated serving dish.


# STIR-FRIED EGGS WITH GREEN BEANS

This is another excellent dish to accompany rice.

Serves 4–5, with other dishes

8–12 ounces green beans
2 cloves garlic
4 eggs
4½ tablespoons vegetable oil

¾ teaspoon salt
1 teaspoon sugar
1 tablespoon dry sherry
1 teaspoon sesame oil

Rinse and trim the beans, blanch them in boiling water for 4–5 minutes, and drain. Crush and chop the garlic. Beat the eggs lightly for 10–15 seconds until blended.

Heat 2½ tablespoons of the oil in a frying pan or wok. When hot, add the beans and salt and stir-fry over medium heat for 1½ minutes. Add the sugar and 4–5 tablespoons water. Continue to stir-fry for a further 2 minutes, or until all the water has evaporated. Push the contents to one side of the pan. Pour the remainder of the oil into the other side of the pan. When hot, pour in the beaten eggs. After 1½ minutes, when the eggs have almost set, turn and stir-fry them for 15 seconds. Bring the beans over to turn and stir with the eggs for half a minute. Sprinkle the contents with sherry and sesame oil. Turn and stir once more, and transfer the contents to a well-heated serving dish.

## CAULIFLOWER EGG FU-YUNG

In China, *fu-yung* is a term that applies to dishes cooked with only the whites of eggs. This is considered to be a more refined dish than the two previous recipes. Being completely white, it is usually served along with darker dishes that have been cooked with soy sauce.

Serves 4–5, with other dishes

1 medium-sized cauliflower
1 small sweet red pepper
5 egg whites
3 teaspoons cornstarch
½ teaspoon salt

3 tablespoons half-and-half or
  light cream
5 tablespoons vegetable oil
4 tablespoons vegetarian stock
1 tablespoon dry sherry

Remove and discard most of the cauliflower stem and break the rest into individual florets. Plunge them into boiling water to parboil for 2 minutes, and drain well. Trim and seed the pepper and cut it into thin strips.

Beat the egg whites together with the cornstarch, salt, and half-

and-half or cream with a fork or chopsticks or a whisk for 2 minutes, until the egg-milk begins to stiffen.

Heat 2½ tablespoons of the oil in a frying pan or wok. When hot, add the cauliflower, pepper, and stock. Stir-fry over high heat for 2 minutes. Reduce the heat to medium-low and push the contents of the pan to one side. Add the remaining oil to the other side of the pan. When hot, add the egg-milk mixture. Stir and scramble for 1½ minutes, or until the egg white begins to set. Bring the vegetable over to mix, stir, and turn with the egg. Sprinkle the contents with sherry and serve.

## PEARL RIVER BOATMEN'S MULTI-LAYER OMELET

Although this dish is not considered a particularly refined one, it is enjoyed by many because of its multiplicity of ingredients, and because it is so different from the ordinary stir-fried dishes.

Serves 6, with other dishes

1 teaspoon salt
6 eggs
3–4 ounces bean sprouts
6 tablespoons vegetable oil
1 clove garlic, crushed and
  chopped
1½ tablespoons soy sauce

3–4 ounces straw mushrooms,
  or button mushrooms
  chopped roughly
2 scallions cut into green and
  white shavings
1½ tablespoons dry sherry

Add the salt to the eggs. Beat them together for 10–15 seconds until blended. Wash the bean sprouts and dry thoroughly.

Heat 2½ tablespoons of the oil in a frying pan or wok. When hot, add the garlic and bean sprouts. Stir-fry over high heat for 1½ minutes, and spread them out evenly over the pan. Pour one-third of the beaten eggs evenly over the pan. As soon as the eggs set, lift the contents in one piece with a wide spatula and transfer to a well-heated serving dish. Pour one-third of the soy sauce over the egg and bean sprouts.

Heat half the remaining oil in the pan. When hot, add the mushrooms and stir-fry over high heat for 1 minute, and spread them evenly over the pan. Pour half the remaining beaten eggs over the mushrooms. As soon as the eggs set, lift the contents out in one piece and place squarely over the egg and bean sprouts that are already in the serving dish.

Pour the remaining oil into the pan. When hot, add the whites of the scallions, stir them around a few times, and spread them evenly over the pan. Pour in the beaten egg and see that it flows evenly over the pan. As soon as the egg sets, sprinkle with the scallion greens and the remaining soy sauce. Lift up the contents in one piece and place on top of the layers of egg and mushroom that are already in the serving dish.

Heat the sherry in the pan. As soon as it boils, pour it over the triple-layer omelet in the serving dish.

## FU-YUNG SAUCE

Chinese *fu-yung* sauce is a white sauce made principally with egg white beaten together with stock and flour. Nonvegetarians usually add minced white fish or white chicken meat, but for a vegetarian version it can simply be made by combining seasoned beaten egg white with cornstarch, vegetarian stock, oil, butter, and milk or cream. It is a useful sauce because it can be used on most vegetables after poaching them briefly in stock or stir-frying them.

Makes 1 cup

| | |
|---|---|
| 4–5 egg whites | 4 tablespoons warm milk |
| 1½ tablespoons butter | 2 tablespoons cream |
| 1 tablespoon cornstarch | 2 tablespoons vegetable oil |
| salt and pepper to taste | |

Beat the egg whites with a whisk for a minute. Add all the remaining ingredients except the oil, and beat them together for a further 1¼ minutes. Heat the vegetable oil in a small pan. When hot, pour in the egg white mixture and stir vigorously with a wooden spoon for 1½ minutes, and the Fu-Yung Sauce is ready for use.

## STIR-FRIED GREEN BEANS IN FU-YUNG SAUCE

This dish presents an attractive green and white mixture. The sauce helps to enrich the vegetable, which after the short cooking should still be crispy. The sauce and the beans make a good dish to go with rice.

Serves 4–5, with other dishes

| | |
|---|---|
| 1 pound green beans | 1 tablespoon light soy sauce |
| 2 cloves garlic | ½ teaspoon salt |
| 2 tablespoons vegetable oil | 1 cup Fu-Yung Sauce (see |
| 4 tablespoons vegetarian stock | above) |

Rinse and trim the beans and cut each one in half. Coarsely crush and chop the garlic.

Heat the oil in a frying pan or wok. When hot, add the beans and garlic and stir-fry over medium heat for 2 minutes. Add the stock, soy sauce, and salt. Continue to stir-fry for 2 minutes, reduce the heat, and continue to cook gently until all the liquid has evaporated. Pour in the Fu-Yung Sauce. Stir and turn the contents together for a further 1½ minutes.

## STIR-FRIED ZUCCHINI IN FU-YUNG SAUCE

Serves 4–5, with other dishes

Repeat the previous recipe, using 12 ounces of zucchini instead of the green beans. The zucchini will need to be trimmed and cut into ½-inch slices. Otherwise the method is precisely the same, except that, since zucchini are a softer vegetable than green beans, the cooking time after the addition of stock can be shortened by 1 minute.

## FU-YUNG CAULIFLOWER WITH CHEESE AND TIANJIN WINTER PICKLE

Cauliflower in Fu-Yung Sauce is an established dish in China. By adding some grated cheese the dish is further enriched, which should endear it to anyone who enjoys eating rice with a rich savory sauce.

Serves 4–5, with other dishes

1 large cauliflower
2 tablespoons winter pickle
2 tablespoons vegetable oil
½ teaspoon salt
2 tablespoons grated cheese
  (cheddar, parmesan, or any
  other hard cheese)

½ cup vegetarian stock
1 vegetarian stock cube
1 cup Fu-Yung Sauce (see
  pages 62–63)

Rinse and trim the cauliflower and break the head into individual florets. Chop the pickle coarsely.

Heat the oil in a saucepan or wok. When hot, add the pickle and stir around a few times, then add the cauliflower and sprinkle on the salt and cheese. Turn the ingredients around in the pan for half a minute. Pour in the stock, add the crumbled stock cube, and bring to a boil. Turn the vegetable around gently in the stock for 2 minutes, reduce the heat, and cover the pan. Cook gently for 3 minutes, then uncover the pan and pour in the Fu-Yung Sauce. Turn the vegetable around in the sauce a few times and continue to cook gently for 2 minutes. Transfer contents to a large serving bowl.

## PEKING STIR-COOKED YELLOW RUNNING EGG

This is a well-established Peking dish—another favorite of rice eaters—which in other cuisines might be considered a sauce or semi-soup dish. Diners eat this by spooning the sauce mixture on top of their own bowls of rice, accompanied by other dishes.

Serves 6–7, with other dishes

3 eggs
3 egg yolks
½ teaspoon salt
1 tablespoon cornstarch
1 cup vegetarian stock
1 cake bean curd
3 ounces straw mushrooms
2 cloves garlic
2½ tablespoons butter

2 tablespoons grated cheese (cheddar, parmesan, or any other hard cheese)
2½ tablespoons vegetable oil
3–4 tablespoons green peas, fresh or frozen
1 tablespoon light soy sauce
2 tablespoons chopped coriander or watercress leaves

Beat the eggs, egg yolks, half the salt, cornstarch, and stock with a whisk for 12–15 seconds until the mixture is blended.

Chop and mash the bean curd. Drain the mushrooms well. Crush and chop the garlic.

Heat the butter in a saucepan. When it has melted, pour in the stock-and-egg mixture. Stir with a wooden spoon over medium heat for 2½ minutes. Add the remaining salt and the grated cheese and continue to stir and mix for a further 2 minutes. Remove from the heat.

Heat the oil in another saucepan. Add the garlic, mushrooms, and green peas and stir over medium heat for 1 minute. Add the mashed bean curd and light soy sauce and continue to stir-fry for a further 2 minutes. Pour in the stock-and-egg mixture from the other pan. Stir and turn all the ingredients together for a further 2 minutes.

Pour the contents of the pan into a large serving bowl and sprinkle with chopped coriander or watercress.

# STEAMED EGG DISHES

## BASIC STEAMED EGGS

Chinese steamed eggs could be said to be similar to Western custard, but in effect they are two very different things. Chinese steamed eggs are almost savory, and they are usually much lighter (probably because no flour or cornstarch is used). Yet, although lighter, they do not flow like cream. They are usually made with clear broth, and seldom with more than two eggs beaten into 2 cups of liquid.

This is an informal dish but one of some refinement. The steamed eggs are spooned into individual rice bowls and consumed alongside heavier and richer dishes.

Serves 4–5, with other dishes

2 eggs
2 cups good vegetarian broth
1 teaspoon salt

1–2 scallions, chopped into
fine shavings
1½ tablespoons soy sauce

Beat the eggs with a fork or chopsticks for 10–15 seconds. Add the broth and salt. Continue to beat and mix for 10–15 seconds until the mixture is blended.

Pour the egg mixture into a large ovenproof bowl. Insert the bowl into a steamer and steam vigorously for 15–17 minutes, until the top of the steamed egg has become somewhat firm.

Remove the bowl from the steamer. Sprinkle the top of the steamed egg with the chopped scallion and soy sauce and serve.

## STEAMED EGGS WITH VEGETABLES AND PICKLES

Serves 5–6, with other dishes

Repeat the previous recipe and add 4–5 medium-sized tomatoes cut into quarters, salt and pepper to taste, 1 tablespoon chopped snow pickle, 1 tablespoon chopped winter pickle, and ½ tablespoon chopped Sichuan Ja Tsai pickle.

Before steaming, put the tomato pieces in the bottom of the bowl and sprinkle them with salt and pepper. Pour in the egg mixture so that the tomato is completely submerged. Insert the bowl into a steamer, and steam vigorously for 17–18 minutes. By this time the surface of the egg mixture should have become firm. Sprinkle with the pickles, followed by the chopped scallion and soy sauce.

## STEAMED EGGS WITH SALT EGGS AND HUNDRED-YEAR-OLD EGGS

The variety of flavors from the three different types of eggs makes this dish quite distinct from any other dish you are likely to encounter.

Serves 5–6, with other dishes

3 hundred-year-old eggs
3 salt eggs
2 eggs
1½ cups good vegetarian
   broth

1 teaspoon salt
1–2 scallions, chopped into
   fine shavings

Clean and remove the shells from the hundred-year-old eggs. Cut each egg into six wedges. Do the same with the salt eggs.

Beat the raw eggs with a fork or chopsticks for 10–15 seconds. Add the broth and salt. Continue to beat and mix for 10–15 seconds until the mixture is blended.

Arrange the wedges of salt egg and hundred-year-old egg over the surface of a large, flat-bottomed, deep-sided heatproof dish. Pour in the beaten egg mixture to half cover the egg pieces. Insert the dish into a steamer and steam vigorously for 10–12 minutes. Sprinkle the scallions on top and serve in the dish in which the eggs were steamed.

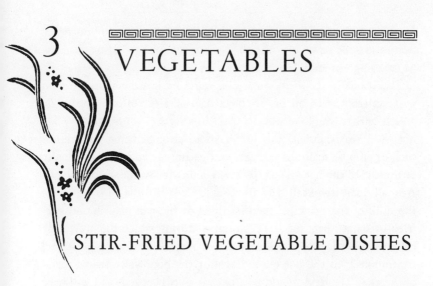

# 3 VEGETABLES

## STIR-FRIED VEGETABLE DISHES

Quick stir-frying has only recently begun to be accepted as a form of cooking in the West, although it has been in wide use in China for over two thousand years. It probably became very popular and was accepted as an established form of cooking because of its speed and convenience—it seldom takes more than a couple of minutes to cut foods up into the required size and shapes, and a further 2–3 minutes, or even less, to stir-fry them in a small amount of oil over high heat. With the arrival of the wok in the West in very recent years, stir-frying rapidly began to catch on, and it has very likely come to stay. Not only is it a very time-saving method of cooking, it is also extremely flexible, capable of producing an almost unlimited range of variations in flavor, color, and shape, and in the possible combinations of foods. It is this speed of cooking and the range and flexibility that make stir-frying so useful and intriguing.

Stir-frying has the further advantage of being a highly nutritious way of cooking. Since the cooking time in stir-frying is extremely short, much more of the food's juices and nutrition can be retained. Besides, in stir-frying, foods are cut into small pieces, slices, or shreds, so many more types of food can be assembled, cooked, and presented in one dish. This gives consumers the advantage of drawing nutrition from a greater range of foods than when confined to eating just one or two single-material bulk-food dishes.

Traditionally, Chinese stir-frying starts by heating no more than 3–4 tablespoons of oil or fat (for a dish of 3–4 portions, normally served with a couple of other dishes) in a frying pan or wok. When hot, 1–3 teaspoons of chopped or sliced strong-tasting vegetables, such as onions, scallions, ginger, and garlic, are added, individually or mixed, to the hot oil for 10–15 seconds to flavor or season the oil. A small quantity of salt may also be added. When the oil is seasoned, the bulk of the principal food is added to the pan or wok and stir-fried over high heat for 1–1½ minutes, during which the previously chopped, sliced, diced, or shredded food material is turned and stirred continuously in the hot oil and against the hot, well-greased metal of the pan. The food should now be two-thirds cooked, and will have released a fair proportion of its natural juices into the pan. At this point the food should be removed with a perforated spoon and put aside for a temporary rest.

The remaining flavored oil and juices left in the pan (not unlike the flavored fat left in a normal roasting pan in Western cooking) are quickly made use of to concoct a sauce. This is achieved by adding to the pan or wok a tablespoon or two of soy sauce (or one of its variants, such as yellow bean paste, hoisin sauce, or *tou-pan* chili-soy paste), chicken (or vegetarian) stock, wine, and a teaspoon or two of sugar (to enrich the sauce). When these ingredients are stirred together in the pan or wok they immediately start to combine, boil, and froth up. A small amount of blended cornstarch (about 2 teaspoons blended in 1½–2 tablespoons water) is now introduced to thicken the sauce. At this point the partially cooked principal food material is returned to the wok and stirred and coated in the sauce. The final turning and stirring over high heat need not last longer than an additional ½–1 minute. A teaspoon of sesame oil and 2 teaspoons of freshly chopped chives or scallions are frequently sprinkled over the food just before serving to enhance its aromatic appeal. This whole process of stir-frying does not normally last for much more than 3–3½ minutes, depending on the quantity of the food to be cooked, the size of the pan or wok used (the bigger, the quicker), the level of heat used, and the size and thickness of the cut foods.

Hence, in Chinese stir-fry cooking, timing and heat control are of paramount importance, and these can only be achieved by putting in time at the stove. But the skill of stir-frying can be acquired and all the mystique surrounding the subject forgotten. Since every dish prepared may require special attention and finesse to cook it to perfection, and since in Chinese cooking stir-fried dishes run into hundreds or thousands, it will require time to cover the mileage. But it should be encouraging to know that the basic skill, or even a feeling of mastery, can be achieved after no more than a dozen attempts. However, a good deal of eating experience, and a knowledge of the range of Chinese cuisine, is important in order to know what should actually be aimed for in any particular Chinese stir-fried dish. What is normally desired is a happy balance of the sweet freshness of the food and its juices and the matured flavor of the seasonings and flavoring agents employed. Harmony is achieved when the two sides are perfectly balanced, especially when the elements of textural and color appeal are conspicuous in the final presentation of the dish.

Through the permutation of food materials and flavoring ingredients used, the number of dishes that can be prepared by stir-frying is almost unlimited. What I shall aim to do in this chapter is to provide recipes that illustrate how some of the popular vegetables are traditionally cooked on their own, or together, in the traditional manner—and thus provide some guidelines as to how to go about stir-frying these vegetables without indulging myself in writing out innumerable recipes to impress readers with the scope and scale of Chinese vegetable cookery.

# STIR-FRIED BEAN SPROUTS WITH GARLIC AND SCALLIONS

Since bean sprouts require no cutting, and are quite edible whether cooked or not, this is one of the easiest and most convenient vegetable dishes to cook.

Serves 3–4, with 1 or 2 other dishes

1 pound bean sprouts
3–4 cloves garlic
3 scallions
3½ tablespoons vegetable oil
1 teaspoon salt

1½ tablespoons vegetarian stock
1 tablespoon light soy sauce
1 tablespoon vinegar
1½ teaspoons sesame oil

Wash and shake the sprouts thoroughly in water. Drain well. Crush and coarsely chop the garlic. Cut the scallions into ¼-inch shavings, separating the white parts from the green.

Heat the oil in a large frying pan or wok. When hot, add the salt, the garlic, and the whites of the scallions and stir them around in the hot oil for 15 seconds. Add the sprouts and turn and stir them together with the other ingredients over high heat for 1 minute. Sprinkle the contents with the stock, soy sauce, and vinegar. Continue to stir-fry over high heat for a further minute. Sprinkle the contents with the scallion greens and the sesame oil. Stir, turn once more, and serve.

# STIR-FRIED GREEN BEANS WITH GARLIC AND CHINESE DRIED MUSHROOMS

The seasoned oil developed from the garlic, mushrooms, stock, bean curd "cheese," soy sauce, and sherry to coat the beans should make the latter extremely flavorful and ideal to consume with quantities of plain cooked rice.

Served 3–4, with 1 or 2 other dishes

1 pound young green beans
3 cloves garlic
3–4 Chinese dried mushrooms
2 teaspoons Chinese red bean curd "cheese"
3 tablespoons vegetarian stock

1½ tablespoons light soy sauce
1 tablespoon sherry
4½ tablespoons vegetable oil
1 teaspoon salt
1½ teaspoons sesame oil

Rinse and trim the beans and cut each one in half. Crush and coarsely chop the garlic. Soak the dried mushrooms in hot water for half an hour. Drain. Remove and discard the stems and coarsely chop the caps. Blend the bean curd "cheese" with the stock, soy sauce, and sherry.

Heat 3½ tablespoons of the oil in a frying pan or wok. When hot, add the salt, garlic, and chopped mushrooms. Stir them in the hot oil for half a minute. Add the beans and stir and turn in the seasoned oil with the mushrooms and garlic for 2 minutes. Add the bean curd "cheese," stock, soy sauce, and sherry mixture. Turn them with the beans quickly over high heat for a further 2 minutes. Sprinkle with the remainder of the vegetable oil and the sesame oil. Turn and stir once more and serve.

73

# STIR-FRIED YOUNG CABBAGE WITH GINGER AND SNOW PICKLES

This cabbage dish is full of wholesome vegetable flavor and is crispy to the bite. Cooked in this way, the cabbage can be consumed in quantity on its own, or with rice and other dishes.

Serves 4–5, with 1 or 2 other dishes

1 young savoy cabbage (about 1½–2 pounds)
3 slices ginger root
2 tablespoons snow pickle
4½ tablespoons vegetable oil
1 teaspoon salt

4–5 tablespoons vegetarian stock
1 tablespoon wine vinegar
2 tablespoons light soy sauce
1½ teaspoons sesame oil

Remove the outer leaves of the cabbage, cut away and discard the stem, and cut the tenderer parts of the cabbage into thin slices. Coarsely chop the ginger and pickle.

Heat the oil in a large frying pan or wok. When hot, add the salt, ginger, and pickle. Stir them in the hot oil for half a minute. Add the cabbage and stir and turn quickly with the other ingredients in the seasoned oil over medium heat for 2 minutes. Add the stock, vinegar, and soy sauce. Continue to turn and stir the ingredients together for 1½ minutes. Spread the cabbage evenly over the pan and leave to cook for a further 1 minute. Turn and scramble the ingredients together and leave to cook for a further minute. Sprinkle with the sesame oil and serve.

## STIR-FRIED HOT AND SOUR CHINESE CABBAGE

Another boon for rice-eaters, who enjoy sharp-tasting foods with the blandness of plain cooked rice.

Serves 3–4, with 1 or 2 other dishes

Repeat the previous recipe, but substitute Chinese cabbage for savoy cabbage, use 2 red chili peppers and 1 dried chili pepper instead of pickles, and increase the quantity of vinegar from 1 tablespoon to 2½ tablespoons. Adopt the same cooking procedure, adding the shredded peppers (after trimming and seeding them) into the hot oil to stir-fry for half a minute before adding the cabbage. The resultant dish will be slightly pink in color and should appeal to all those who enjoy spicy food.

## SWEET AND SOUR CABBAGE

This is another appealing dish to have with rice. Either regular or savoy cabbage can be used. For those who enjoy spicy food, ½ tablespoon of chili sauce may be added to the ingredients for the sauce.

Serves 4–5, with other dishes

1½–2 pounds cabbage
2 slices ginger root
4 tablespoons vegetable oil
1 teaspoon salt

4 tablespoons vegetarian stock
SAUCE:
2 tablespoons sugar
3½ tablespoons wine vinegar

1½ tablespoons light soy
   sauce
1½ tablespoons tomato paste
2 tablespoons orange juice

1 tablespoon cornstarch
   blended in 3 tablespoons
   water

Cut the cabbage into thin slices after removing the outer leaves and discarding the stem. Cut the ginger into fine shreds, and mix the ingredients for the sauce until well blended.

Heat the oil in a large frying pan or wok. When hot, add the shredded ginger and salt and stir for a quarter of a minute. Add the cabbage and stir and turn in the seasoned oil until every piece is well coated and lubricated. Spread the cabbage evenly over the pan or wok. Sprinkle it with stock. As the stock bubbles and froths, turn and stir the cabbage over high heat for 1½ minutes. Pour the sauce evenly over the pan. Stir and turn the cabbage over a few times until the sauce begins to thicken and becomes glistening and glossy.

## STIR-FRIED SPINACH WITH GARLIC AND CHINESE BEAN CURD ''CHEESE''

Although a simple dish by ordinary culinary standards, it often turns out to be the most appealing on the menu of any reputable restaurant in China or abroad. What makes it appealing is the unmistakable character and quality of the vegetable cooked and eaten in bulk.

Serves 3–4, with 1 or 2 other dishes

1 pound young spinach
4 cloves garlic
4½ tablespoons vegetable oil
1 teaspoon salt

½ tablespoon bean curd
   ''cheese''
1 tablespoon light soy sauce
1 teaspoon sesame oil

Wash and dry the spinach thoroughly. Remove and discard the stems and any discolored leaves. Cut into 1-inch slices. Crush and coarsely chop the garlic.

Heat 4 tablespoons of the oil in a large frying pan or wok. When hot, add the garlic and salt and stir over medium heat for a quarter of a minute. Add the bean curd "cheese" and stir and mix the ingredients together for another half minute. Add the spinach and turn and mix evenly with the garlic, "cheese," and seasoned oil. Continue to turn and mix over medium heat for 1½ minutes. Add the soy sauce, the remaining ½ tablespoon of vegetable oil, and the sesame oil. Stir and turn for half a minute over high heat and serve.

# STIR-FRIED ASPARAGUS WITH GARLIC

The asparagus should be bright green, glistening, and still crunchy when served. The appeal of this dish lies in the fullness of its distinctive vegetable flavor.

Serves 3–4, with 1 or 2 other dishes

1–1¼ pounds young
   asparagus
2 cloves garlic
4½ tablespoons vegetable oil
1 teaspoon salt

1½ teaspoons sugar
1 tablespoon soy sauce
3 tablespoons vegetarian stock
1 tablespoon dry sherry

Remove and discard the tough white root ends of the asparagus spears and cut each spear diagonally into 2-inch sections. Crush and coarsely chop the garlic.

Heat the oil in a frying pan or wok. When hot, add the salt, garlic, and asparagus. Turn them in the hot oil over high heat for 2 minutes. Add the sugar, soy sauce, stock, and sherry. Stir and turn the vegetable over in the sauce several times. Reduce the heat to low and spread the vegetable evenly over the pan. Leave to cook for 3–3½ minutes, until all the liquid has evaporated. Stir, turn once more, and serve.

## STIR-FRIED BROCCOLI WITH GARLIC

This is another green, crunchy vegetable dish very similar to the previous one in appearance and appeal. The sweet, fresh vegetable taste is thrown into contrast by the sauce's savory saltiness.

Serves 3–4, with 1 or 2 other dishes

1–1¼ pounds broccoli
2 cloves garlic
2 teaspoons bean curd "cheese"
2½ tablespoons vegetarian stock

1 tablespoon soy sauce
1 tablespoon dry sherry
3½ tablespoons vegetable oil
1 teaspoon salt
1½ teaspoons sugar

Trim off the end of the broccoli stem and cut the rest slantwise into ¾-inch slices. Parboil in boiling water for 2 minutes and drain well. Break the broccoli head into individual 1–1½-inch florets. Crush and coarsely chop the garlic. Mix the "cheese" with the stock, soy sauce, and sherry until well blended.

Heat the oil in a frying pan or wok. When hot, add the salt and garlic. Stir them around for 20 seconds and add both the sliced stems and the florets of the broccoli. Stir and turn them around in the hot oil with the garlic for 1 minute, until every piece of vegetable is well coated with the seasoned oil. Sprinkle the broccoli with the sugar, then pour the "cheese"-stock-soy-sherry mixture over it. Turn and stir the sauce until every piece of vegetable is evenly covered. Reduce the heat to low and cook gently for 2½ minutes. Turn and stir once more and serve.

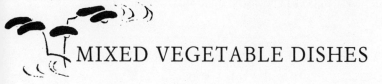

# MIXED VEGETABLE DISHES

These are just a few examples of the many familiar combinations.

## STIR-FRIED LIMA BEANS WITH STRAW MUSHROOMS

A very satisfying dish to spoon into your rice bowl and eat with mouthfuls of rice. Serve in a deep-sided dish or a serving bowl.

Serves 5–6, with other dishes

8–10 ounces fresh or frozen lima beans
6–8 ounces canned straw mushrooms
4–4½ tablespoons vegetable oil
1 teaspoon salt

½ teaspoon sugar
¾ tablespoon light soy sauce
1½ teaspoons sesame oil
2½ teaspoons cornstarch blended in 2 tablespoons water

Parboil the beans in boiling water for 2½–3 minutes and drain. Drain the straw mushrooms, reserving 4 tablespoons of the mushroom water.

Heat the oil in a saucepan or wok. When hot, add the beans and stir-fry over medium heat for 2 minutes. Add the straw mushrooms, salt, and sugar, and stir-fry them together for 1½ minutes. Add the soy sauce, the 4 tablespoons mushroom water, and the sesame oil. Stir and turn all the ingredients together for a further 2 minutes. Finally add the blended cornstarch. Continue mixing and turning until the sauce thickens and turns somewhat translucent.

## STIR-FRIED FAVA BEANS WITH PICKLES

The majority of Chinese dishes of this type are meant to be eaten with rice. In this case the richness of the purée gives body to the dish and the oil in the dish provides the "lubrication" necessary when eating quantities of rice.

Serves 4–5, with 1 or 2 other dishes

| | |
|---|---|
| 5–6 ounces dried fava beans or dried split green peas | 3–4 ounces bean sprouts |
| | 4 tablespoons vegetable oil |
| 4 tablespoons snow pickle | 1 teaspoon sugar |
| 1½ tablespoons Sichuan Ja Tsai pickle | 1½ teaspoons sesame oil |
| | 1 tablespoon soy sauce |

Soak beans (or peas) overnight in cold water. Rinse under running water. Place in a saucepan, bring to a boil, and simmer gently for 40–45 minutes. Drain, reserving ½ cup of the water. Coarsely chop both types of pickles. Mash the beans (or peas) into a purée. Cut the bean sprouts into ¼-inch shavings.

Heat 1½ tablespoons of the vegetable oil in a saucepan or wok. When hot, add the pickles and stir-fry for 1 minute. Add the remaining oil and the sugar, followed by the vegetable purée. Stir over low-medium heat for 1½ minutes. Pour in the reserved cooking water and the sprouts and continue to stir and mix for 2½ minutes. Add the sesame oil and soy sauce and continue to cook and stir gently for a further half minute before serving.

# STIR-FRIED ZUCCHINI WITH BRAISED BAMBOO SHOOTS AND BUTTON MUSHROOMS

The combined effect of braised bamboo shoots, pickle, and chili should give this dish a pronounced savory flavor, making it another favorite for rice eaters.

Serves 4–5, with 1 or 2 other dishes

12 ounces zucchini

8 ounces braised bamboo shoots (available canned and marinated)

8 ounces button mushrooms

2 tablespoons snow pickle

2 small dried chilies

4 tablespoons vegetable oil

1 tablespoon light soy sauce

3 tablespoons vegetarian stock

1½ teaspoons sesame oil

Rinse and trim the zucchini and cut slantwise into ½-inch sections. Cut the bamboo shoots into similar-sized pieces. Clean and trim the mushrooms and cut through stem and cap into halves. Chop the pickle. Trim, seed, and chop the chilies.

Heat the oil in a frying pan or wok. When hot, add the pickles and chilies. Stir-fry for 1 minute. Add the bamboo shoots, zucchini, and mushrooms. Continue to stir-fry over medium heat for 3 minutes. Add the soy sauce and stock, which should start to boil and bubble immediately. Stir and turn the ingredients in the bubbling sauce for 1 more minute, add the sesame oil, and serve.

# STIR-FRIED SNOW PEAS WITH BABY CORN, DRIED MUSHROOMS, AND WOOD EARS

This is a colorful dish, with the bright green of the snow peas, the black of the wood ears and dried mushrooms, and the yellow of the baby corn, all contrasting sharply in color and texture.

Serves 5–6, with 1 or 2 other dishes

8 ounces snow peas
5–6 ounces canned baby
  corn
4–5 medium-sized Chinese
  dried mushrooms
2 slices ginger root
3–4 tablespoons dried wood
  ears

2 teaspoons bean curd
  "cheese"
2 tablespoons vegetarian stock
3½ tablespoons vegetable oil
¾ teaspoon salt
1 teaspoon sugar
1 tablespoon light soy sauce
1 tablespoon dry sherry

Trim and cut each snow pea slantwise into halves. Drain the baby corn. Soak the dried mushrooms in hot water for half an hour. Drain. Remove and discard the stems and cut each cap into quarters. Shred the ginger. Soak the wood ears for 4–5 minutes, rinse, and drain. Mix the bean curd "cheese" with the stock until well blended.

Heat the oil in a frying pan or wok. When hot, add the ginger and mushrooms and stir-fry for 1 minute, followed by the snow peas, salt, and wood ears. Stir and turn them together over medium heat for 1½ minutes. Add the baby corn and sugar, then pour in the soy sauce, the sherry, and the "cheese"-stock mixture. This should immediately froth up into a bubbling sauce mixture. Turn the contents quickly in the sauce over high heat and stir constantly for 1½ more minutes. By this time most of the moisture will have evaporated, and the sauce will have formed a savory coating on the vegetables.

#  BRAISED VEGETABLE DISHES

Much more use seems to be made of the stems of vegetables in Chinese cooking than in Western. When vegetable stems are cooked with care they can often be just as appealing and palatable, if not even more satisfying, than the leaves and tops. In the majority of cases the stems require longer cooking to tenderize them than could be achieved through a couple of minutes of stir-frying. Hence the cooking method most often used in cooking hard roots or stems is *braising*.

In China, braising can be a simple continuation of the stir-frying process, where some stock and sauce are added and the heat reduced so that the vegetable can be cooked slowly, partly in its own juice and partly in the stock and sauce added. It may be 10–12 minutes before the vegetable is tender.

Braising also involves cooking the harder vegetables along with flavoring ingredients, such as pickles and sauces, over a gentle heat for a good period of time (20–30 minutes). This results in the chunkier cuts of vegetables being "dry cooked" (rather like pot roasting) until tenderized and made flavorful by the slow action of the added sauces and the lengthy cooking of the vegetables in their own juices.

Effective braising can also be achieved by cooking hard vegetables over high heat in ample sauce and stock through a process of rapid reduction. When nearly all the moisture and liquid have evaporated, after 20 minutes or more of vigorous boiling or stewing, the vegetables will have become suitably tenderized and coated by a sauce, the ingredients for which can be varied and made up as the cooking proceeds.

Whichever process is used, braised vegetables can be used extensively in stir-frying with the tenderer leaf (or quick-cooked) vegetables to produce a whole new range of vegetable dishes. This is more or less how Chinese dishes multiply, giving rise to new horizons which seem to be never-ending.

83

Most people are aware of the pleasure of eating the leaves of fresh, crispy vegetables, but few have achieved the cultivated taste and enjoyment of biting into a thick chunk of crunchy vegetable such as a wedge of triangularly cut turnip, carrot, or bamboo shoot, when the teeth sink through the outer surface of the chunky vegetable made savory by the long period of cooking in a sauce. Most Chinese gastronomes have gained this cultivated taste from eating all different types of bamboo shoots: winter bamboo shoots, bamboo shoot tips, chunky bamboo shoots, pickled bamboo shoots, soy-braised marinated bamboo shoots, and so on.

This inevitably extended to all other thick, crunchy vegetables, such as carrots, turnips, asparagus, broccoli and cauliflower stems, parsnips, squash, winter melons, cucumbers, and celery. These vegetables are cooked in different ways—some soy-braised with or without sugar and chili, others simmered in stock or quickly stir-fried—but all are thick-cut into varying shapes and sizes, to be cooked together with leaf vegetables, noodles, or transparent pea- or bean-starch noodles (which can withstand lengthy cooking without becoming mushy). A whole genre of dishes consequently stems from the many possible combinations.

Normally in Chinese cooking the cutting of supplementary ingredients should follow the shape and size of the principal ingredient of the dish (so that in the cooking of a noodle dish, for example, the supplementary ingredients and materials should all be cut into thin strips like noodles). In some cases, however, materials and ingredients are purposely cut into contrasting sizes and shapes to provide variation, especially when they are able to retain much of their original flavor because of their thickness. These larger cuts of chunky vegetables, cooked in different ways and for different lengths of time, have their own special function in the ever-varying combination of materials and ingredients characteristic of Chinese cooking.

# MIXED STIR-FRY OF "TWO WINTERS" WITH ZUCCHINI

This is a very tasty and crunchy dish that can be eaten as a starter, as a snack accompanied by wine, or with plain rice.

Serves 4–5, with 1 or 2 other dishes

4–5 ounces winter bamboo
    shoots
6 large Chinese dried winter
    mushrooms
1½ medium-sized zucchini
3 slices ginger root
3½ tablespoons vegetable oil
¾ teaspoon salt

1 teaspoon sugar
3 tablespoons vegetarian stock
1 tablespoon light soy sauce
1 tablespoon dry sherry
1 tablespoon margarine or
    butter
1 tablespoon sesame oil

Cut the bamboo shoots into 1½–1¾-inch wedges. Soak the dried mushrooms in hot water for half an hour and drain, reserving 3 tablespoons of the mushroom water. Remove and discard the stems and cut the caps into quarters. Trim off the ends of the zucchini and cut slantwise into ½-inch slices. Shred the ginger.

Heat the oil in a frying pan or wok. When hot, add the ginger and mushrooms. Stir-fry over high heat for 1 minute. Add the bamboo shoots, salt, sugar, mushroom water, and stock. Continue to turn and stir for 1 minute. Cover the pan or wok, reduce the heat, and cook gently for 2 minutes. Remove the cover and add the zucchini, soy sauce, sherry, and margarine or butter. Stir-fry all the ingredients together for a further 1½ minutes. Sprinkle with the sesame oil and serve.

# STIR-FRY OF TWO BRAISED AND TWO SIMMERED SHREDDED VEGETABLES

One of the enjoyments of eating this dish is the multiple texture and flavor sensation it gives when biting through the strands and threads of the four different vegetables.

*Serves 4–5, with other dishes*

2 medium-sized young carrots
4–5 ounces bamboo shoots
3 slices ginger root
3 medium-sized dried
   mushrooms
2 stalks celery
6-inch section medium-sized
   cucumber
3 tablespoons vegetable oil

1 teaspoon sugar
1 tablespoon yellow bean
   sauce
4 tablespoons vegetarian stock
1 tablespoon soy sauce
1 tablespoon margarine or
   butter
1 teaspoon sesame oil

Clean and cut the carrots, bamboo shoots, and ginger into matchstick shreds. Soak the mushrooms in hot water for half an hour and drain, reserving the water. Remove and discard the stems and cut the caps into similar shreds. Clean and cut the celery and cucumber into 1½-by-¼-inch strips.

Heat the oil in a frying pan or wok. When hot, add the ginger and mushrooms and stir-fry over high heat for 1 minute. Add the carrots, bamboo shoots, mushroom water, sugar, and yellow bean sauce. Turn and stir the ingredients. Reduce the heat and leave the contents to braise and simmer together for 3 minutes, turning them over now and then.

Heat the stock and soy sauce together in a pan or wok. When the mixture boils, add the celery and cucumber. Turn them in the sauce and simmer for 2 minutes, by which time the liquid in the pan or wok should nearly have dried up.

Transfer the contents of the second pan or wok into the first. Add the margarine or butter and the sesame oil. Stir-fry the contents together for a further 1 minute and serve.

## FOUR SOY-BRAISED CHUNKY VEGETABLES WITH PICKLES

This is a dish of rich, glistening, chunky vegetables, often used in China to nibble, chew, and crunch in the mouth while drinking wine. It can also be consumed with plain boiled rice.

*Serves 4–5, with other dishes*

2 large young carrots
4 ounces turnips
4 ounces parsnips
4 ounces bamboo shoots
1½ tablespoons snow pickle
1 tablespoon Sichuan Ja Tsai pickle
4 tablespoons vegetable oil
1 tablespoon sugar
1½ tablespoons yellow bean sauce

1½ tablespoons soy sauce
2 teaspoons chili sauce
½ cup vegetarian stock
1 tablespoon dry sherry
1 tablespoon margarine or butter
1½ teaspoons sesame oil
1½ tablespoons chopped parsley

Scrape or peel the carrots, turnips, and parsnips and cut them into 1½–2-inch wedges. Cut the bamboo shots into similar pieces. Coarsely chop the pickles.

Heat the oil in a heavy saucepan or casserole. When hot, add the pickles and stir for half a minute. Add all the vegetables and stir and turn in the seasoned oil for 1 minute. Add the sugar, yellow bean sauce, soy sauce, chili sauce, and stock. Bring the contents to a boil and turn around a few times. Cover the pan or casserole with a lid. Reduce the heat and leave to braise and simmer for 5–6 minutes. Remove the lid and turn the contents over several times. Cover again and braise and simmer for a further 5–6 minutes. Remove the lid once more and add the sherry, margarine or butter, and sesame oil. Raise the heat to high and stir-fry until nearly all the sauce that coats the vegetables has thickened to a glaze. Sprinkle with chopped parsley and serve.

## SICHUAN HOT-BRAISED STIR-FRIED EGGPLANT

This is a hot, spicy dish, typical of the province of Sichuan, and is very suitable for eating with copious amounts of plain boiled rice. Most of these provincial dishes are "dishes for the masses," which are meant for hearty eating, but over the years they have assumed a refined and classical status.

Serves 4–5, with other dishes

2 medium-sized eggplants
2 slices ginger root
3–4 dried red chilies
2 scallions
4 tablespoons vegetable oil
1½ tablespoons yellow bean sauce
2 teaspoons sugar
½ teaspoon salt

4 tablespoons vegetarian stock
1 tablespoon soy sauce
1½ tablespoons Sichuan chili-soy paste
1½ tablespoons wine vinegar
2½ teaspoons cornstarch blended in 2 tablespoons water
1 teaspoon sesame oil

Remove the stem ends of the eggplants. Cut the eggplants into strips approximately ½ by ½ by 2½ inches. Shred the ginger. Trim, seed, and coarsely chop the chilies. Cut the scallions into ¼-inch shavings, separating the whites from the greens.

Heat the oil in a wok or heavy saucepan. When hot, add the ginger, the chilies, and the whites of the scallions. Stir-fry for 1 minute. Add the yellow bean sauce, sugar, salt, stock, and eggplant. Raise the heat to high and turn and stir the contents together in the bubbling sauce for 1½ minutes. Reduce the heat to low and simmer gently, covered, for 3 minutes. Remove the lid and add the soy sauce, chili-soy paste, and vinegar. Stir and turn over high heat for 1 minute. Pour in the blended cornstarch. Stir and turn to mix in with the other ingredients. As soon as the blended cornstarch thickens and turns translucent, sprinkle with the scallion greens and sesame oil and serve.

## STIR-FRIED TRANSPARENT BEAN-STARCH NOODLES WITH LILY BUDS, MUSHROOMS, WOOD EARS, AND BRAISED STEMS OF BROCCOLI AND HEART OF CABBAGE

Transparent bean-starch noodles are a great absorber of liquid. Their weight is increased at least four times when soaked in water. However, unlike wheat-starch noodles, they are not eaten as bulk food or on their own but usually as a supplementary ingredient for cooking with other foods. As such, and because of their ability to absorb the flavors of other ingredients, they play a unique part in augmenting savory dishes and providing bulk dishes to accompany rice (for example, by adding gravy to transparent noodles a dish of considerable dimension and savoriness can be created at very little cost that can be as appealing as another dish costing ten times as much). It is a dish that is often seen on family dining tables.

Serves 5–6, with other dishes

3–4 ounces dry transparent
  noodles
2 lily buds
3 tablespoons wood ears
2 slices ginger root
6 medium-sized dried
  mushrooms
2 tablespoons snow pickle
2 tablespoons winter pickle

3½ ounces broccoli stems
3½ ounces heart and stem of
  cabbage
3½ tablespoons vegetable oil
1 teaspoon salt
1 cup vegetarian stock
1 tablespoon soy sauce
1 vegetarian stock cube
1 teaspoon sesame oil

Soak the noodles and lily buds in warm water for 5 minutes and drain. Cut the lily buds into 1½-inch sections. Soak the wood ears in warm water for 3 minutes, rinse under running water, and cut into roughly 2-inch pieces. Shred the ginger. Soak the mushrooms in hot water for half an hour, drain, remove and discard the stems, and cut the caps into matchstick shreds. Coarsely chop the pickles. Cut the broccoli and cabbage into nice neat 1½-by-½-inch pieces.

Heat the oil in a saucepan or wok. When hot, add the ginger, dried mushrooms, salt, lily buds, and pickles. Stir over medium heat for 1½ minutes. Add the noodles and stir and turn with the other ingredients in the seasoned oil for 2½ minutes.

Meanwhile, heat the stock in a separate pan or wok. When it begins to boil, add the broccoli stems and heart of cabbage. Bring back to a boil and add the soy sauce and crumbled stock cube. Reduce the heat and simmer gently for 5 minutes, or until half the liquid has evaporated.

Transfer the contents of the second pan or wok to the first. Raise the heat to high. Turn and stir all the ingredients together for 2½ minutes. Sprinkle with sesame oil and serve.

# STIR-FRIED AND BRAISED ASPARAGUS TIPS WITH BAMBOO SHOOT SPEARS AND READY-SOY-BRAISED BAMBOO SHOOTS AND SNOW PICKLE

The principal ingredients of this dish only need to be cooked for a short time. It is highly crunchy and should appeal to the texturally conscious gastronome. In China this dish is frequently used to entertain wine drinkers.

Serves 5–6, with other dishes

3 slices ginger root
1 pound fresh young
  asparagus
8 ounces bamboo shoot spears
5 ounces canned ready-braised
  bamboo shoots
3 tablespoons vegetable oil
2 tablespoons Sichuan Ja Tsai
  pickle

3 tablespoons snow pickle
½ teaspoon salt
2 teaspoons sugar
½ cup vegetarian stock
1 tablespoon yellow bean
  sauce
2 teaspoons bean curd
  "cheese"
1½ tablespoons dry sherry

Cut the ginger into shreds. Rinse and trim the asparagus spears and cut into approximately 3-inch lengths. Cut the bamboo shoot spears and braised bamboo shoots into approximately the same lengths.

Heat the oil in a large frying pan or wok. When hot, add the ginger, pickles, and salt and stir them in the hot oil for half a minute. Add the asparagus and stir for 1 minute. Add the bamboo shoot spears and sugar and pour in the stock. Bring to a boil, reduce the heat, and cook gently for 3–4 minutes. Add the braised bamboo shoots, turn the contents over several times, and simmer for a further 2 minutes. By this time the liquid in the pan or wok should be reduced to less than one quarter. Add the yellow bean sauce, bean curd "cheese," and sherry. Raise the heat to high and turn and stir the contents for 1 more minute, which should further reduce the sauce to a mere glaze.

## BRAISED RED-COOKED CABBAGE

This dish should be served in a deep-sided dish or a large bowl. It is highly savory, and because of its sweet, appealing flavor people are inclined to eat more vegetable than they normally do. The oil and fat combine to add to the succulence of the dish.

Serves 5–6, with other dishes

1 medium-sized white cabbage (about 2–3 pounds)
3 slices ginger root
4 tablespoons vegetable oil
4 tablespoons vegetarian stock

2 tablespoons light soy sauce
1½ tablespoons dark soy sauce
1 tablespoon sugar
1½ tablespoons margarine or butter

Remove the tough lower stem of the cabbage. Cut the cabbage first into slices 1 inch thick and then into 2-inch pieces. Shred the ginger.

Heat the oil in a heavy saucepan or casserole. Add the ginger and stir for half a minute. Add all the cabbage and turn in the seasoned oil over medium heat for 1 minute. Add the stock, light and dark soy sauce, and sugar. Continue to stir and turn the contents for 1 minute. Cover the pan or casserole, reduce the heat to low, and simmer for 5 minutes. Remove the lid, add the margarine or butter, and turn and stir the contents once more to see that the cabbage is evenly sauced and "lubricated." Simmer gently for a further 5 minutes. By this time the cabbage should be sufficiently cooked. It should have become both rich and tender, although some parts will remain appealingly crunchy.

## WHITE-COOKED CABBAGE

This is another highly savory dish. As in the previous recipe, it should be served in a deep-sided dish or a large bowl. Because of the succulence of the dish and its rich vegetable flavor, it is ideal for consuming with rice, and it encourages people to eat cabbage in quantity with enjoyment.

### Serves 5–6, with other dishes

1 medium-sized white or Chinese Tientsin cabbage (about 2½–3 pounds)
2 slices ginger root
1 tablespoon Sichuan Ja Tsai pickle
2 red chilies
4 tablespoons vegetable oil

1½ teaspoons salt
4 tablespoons vegetarian stock
1 tablespoon light soy sauce
1 vegetarian stock cube
4 tablespoons milk
1½ tablespoons margarine or butter

Remove the tougher lower stem of the cabbage. Cut the cabbage first into slices 1 inch thick and then into 2-inch pieces. Shred the ginger and pickle. Trim, seed, and shred the chilies.

Heat the oil in a saucepan or casserole. Add the ginger, pickle, and chilies. Stir for 1 minute. Add the cabbage, salt, stock, and soy sauce. Stir and turn them together over medium heat for 1½ minutes, or until the cabbage is well sauced and "lubricated." Cover the pan or casserole and cook gently over low heat for 5 minutes. Remove the lid and add the crumbled stock cube, milk, and margarine or butter. Stir and turn the contents to mix the ingredients evenly, replace the lid, and simmer gently for a further 5 minutes.

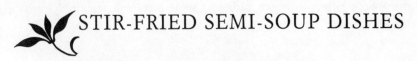

# STIR-FRIED SEMI-SOUP DISHES

This is a distinct category of dish in Chinese cuisine, and one that is seldom seen in Western cooking—mainly because Chinese meals are centered around rice, which is made easier and more appealing to eat by the ample provision of sauce and savory soup dishes.

Preparing these dishes usually starts with stir-frying. The Chinese believe that it is necessary to cook dried, pickled, salted, or strong-tasting ingredients in hot oil first in order to "liberate" their flavors, and that it is only after the flavors have been liberated that the other ingredients and materials should be added to produce the bulk of the dish. The following few recipes should illustrate this method.

## STIR-FRIED SEMI-SOUP DISH OF MUSHROOMS, PICKLES, CUCUMBER, AND CABBAGE

Serve in a deep-sided dish or large bowl. This is a rich vegetable dish, suitable for eating with copious amounts of rice.

Serves 5–6, with other dishes

1½ tablespoons dried salted turnips
3 ounces braised and marinated bamboo shoots
6-inch section medium-sized cucumber
8 ounces Chinese Tientsin cabbage
3 ounces baby corn
4–6 medium-sized Chinese dried mushrooms
3½ tablespoons vegetable oil
1½ tablespoons Sichuan Ja Tsai pickle, shredded
1½ tablespoons snow pickle, chopped

2 tablespoons winter pickle,
  ready shredded
1 cup vegetarian stock
1 vegetarian stock cube
3 ounces bean sprouts

1 teaspoon salt
1 tablespoon light soy sauce
1½ teaspoons sesame oil
2 tablespoons coriander
  leaves, chopped

Shred the turnips. Cut the braised bamboo shoots into 2-inch sections and the cucumber (including the skin) into similar-sized pieces. Cut the cabbage into slices ½ inch thick. Drain the baby corn. Soak the mushrooms in hot water, remove and discard the stems, and cut the caps into shreds.

Heat the oil in a saucepan or casserole. When hot, add the pickles and mushrooms. Stir-fry for 1½ minutes over medium heat. Add the bamboo shoots, turnips, and cabbage and pour in the stock. Bring to a boil, add the crumbled stock cube, and simmer for 5 minutes. Add the bean sprouts, cucumber, baby corn, salt, and soy sauce. Turn and stir them together and continue to cook gently for 5 minutes. Sprinkle with the sesame oil and chopped coriander leaves and serve.

## STIR-FRIED SEMI-SOUP DISH OF MUSHROOMS, PICKLES, BRAISED BAMBOO SHOOTS, BROCCOLI, TRANSPARENT NOODLES, AND SEAWEED

Serves 5–6, with other dishes

4–5 medium-sized dried
  mushrooms
2 tablespoons snow pickle

3–5 ounces broccoli or broccoli stems

3–4 ounces braised bamboo shoots

2 ounces dried kelp (available from Chinese foodstores)

1 ounce hair seaweed (available from Chinese foodstores)

3 ounces dry transparent bean-starch noodles

3½ tablespoons vegetable oil

1 cup vegetarian stock

1 vegetarian stock cube

2–3 ounces bean sprouts

1 teaspoon salt

1½ tablespoons light soy sauce

2–3 sheets purple seaweed (available from Chinese foodstores)

1 teaspoon sesame oil

Soak the mushrooms in hot water for half an hour, remove and discard the stems, and shred the caps. Coarsely chop the pickle. Cut the broccoli or broccoli stems and bamboo shoots into 1½-by-½-inch sections. Soak the kelp for 15 minutes, drain, and cut into 2-by-½-inch strips. Soak the hair seaweed and noodles for 5 minutes and drain.

Heat the oil in a large saucepan or casserole. When hot, add the mushrooms, pickle, and braised bamboo shoots. Stir for 1½ minutes. Add the broccoli and kelp and stir all the ingredients together for a further 1½ minutes. Pour in the stock and add the crumbled stock cube, noodles, bean sprouts, hair seaweed, salt, and soy sauce. Stir them all together and bring to a boil. Reduce the heat and simmer gently for 5–6 minutes. Serve in a deep-sided dish or large bowl. Sprinkle the top of the dish with crumbled purple seaweed and sesame oil.

# STIR-FRIED SEMI-SOUP DISH OF MUSHROOMS, CUCUMBER, BAMBOO SHOOTS, ASPARAGUS SPEARS, WINTER MELON, GREEN PEAS, TRANSPARENT NOODLES, AND BEAN SPROUTS, SERVED IN A MELON BOWL (TUNG KUA CHUNG)

This is quite a classic dish which is usually served at a party meal. Serving the dish in a natural vegetable bowl doubly emphasizes the vegetarian nature of the dish.

*Serve with other dishes for a party meal*

Repeat the previous recipe, substituting 2 tablespoons shredded Sichuan Ja Tsai pickle for the snow pickle and 4–6 ounces straw mushrooms for the various seaweeds. Serve in a large, hollowed-out winter melon, using a quarter of the melon flesh in the dish.

After stir-frying the various ingredients together and simmering them in stock, pour all the contents into the melon. It is customary in China to place the whole melon in a steamer for 7–8 minutes before serving. For serving, it is best to sit the melon in a large bowl.

# SEMI-SOUP DISH OF STIR-FRIED PICKLES, SCALLIONS, AND PURÉE OF BEANS, WITH BEETS, GINGKO NUTS, AND CROUTONS

Serve in a deep-sided dish or a large bowl. This dish is appealing to rice eaters mainly because of its rich, creamy savoriness, which goes well with plain rice; the beets and croutons provide the textural variation.

Serves 5–6, with other dishes

3 scallions
3–4 ounces lima beans
3–4 ounces white beans
2 ounces gingko nuts or lotus
   seeds
3 ounces cooked beets
4–5 tablespoons croutons (or
   their Chinese equivalent,
   crispy rice scrapings)
3 tablespoons vegetable oil

3 tablespoons chopped snow
   pickle
2 slices chopped ginger root
½ teaspoon salt
1 cup vegetarian stock
1 vegetarian stock cube
2 tablespoons butter or margarine
4 tablespoons half-and-half or
   light cream

Cut the scallions into ¼-inch shavings, separating the white parts from the green. Boil the lima beans and white beans for 1 hour and purée in a blender or food processor. Rinse and wash the gingko nuts. Cut the beets into cubes the size of half a sugar lump. Prepare the croutons by frying cubed bread or dried rice scrapings in hot oil until crisp (these should be freshly prepared before sprinkling over the soup).

Heat the oil in a saucepan. Add the pickles, ginger, salt, and the white parts of the scallions. Stir for 1 minute. Add the stock, stock cube, and gingko nuts. Bring to a boil and stir for 1 minute. Add the purée of beans and the butter or margarine. Bring to a gentle boil and simmer gently for 5–6 minutes. Stir the beets and the half-and-half or cream into the soup and bring back to a simmer. Sprinkle with crispy croutons or rice scrapings immediately before serving.

# SEMI-SOUP DISH OF STIR-FRIED PICKLES, SCALLIONS, AND GREEN PEAS WITH LIMA BEANS

Although this is a simple dish to cook, it is appealing to the rice eater for the same reason as the previous recipe. It should be served in a deep-sided dish or a large bowl for the diners to scoop or spoon onto the rice in their rice bowls. Since the foods in most Chinese stir-fried dishes are cut into strips, slices, or cubes or left in chunky pieces, these rich, creamy dishes that can be spooned onto the rice provide a welcome change.

Serves 5–6, with other dishes

3 tablespoons snow pickle
3 scallions
8 ounces lima beans
3 tablespoons vegetable oil
4 ounces fresh or frozen green
   peas

1 teaspoon salt
1 cup vegetarian stock
1 vegetarian stock cube
4 tablespoons half-and-half
1½ tablespoons butter or
   margarine

Coarsely chop the pickle. Cut the scallions into ⅛-inch shavings, separating the whites from the greens. Soak the beans for 3–4 hours, boil in water for 1 hour, and purée in a blender or food processor.

Heat the oil in a saucepan or casserole. When hot, add the white of the scallions and the pickle. Stir over medium heat for 1 minute. Add the peas and salt and stir the ingredients together for 1½ minutes. Pour in the stock and add the crumbled stock cube. When the latter has dissolved and the contents start to boil, add the puréed beans. Bring to a gentle boil, stirring all the time. Simmer and stir for 3 minutes. Add the half-and-half and the butter or margarine, sprinkle with the scallion greens, and serve.

# STEAMED VEGETABLE DISHES

Steaming as a method of cooking is much more widely used in China than in the West. There is always a big pan or cauldron of boiling water in a Chinese kitchen, due to the vast amount of rice that is cooked daily, and the steam generated can be used to cook other foods. You will seldom see an oven in a Chinese kitchen, which means that very few dishes are roasted, while innumerable dishes are steamed. However, because of the high water content of most vegetables, where the aim during the process of cooking is more to reduce the water content and therefore to concentrate the flavor, rather than to increase it through a process of wet-cooking (i.e. boiling or steaming), steaming is not a method widely adopted for cooking vegetables. It is used much more as part of another process: for example, marinating and steaming, stir-frying and steaming, steaming and dousing with blazing oil. Using hot oil in the process of steaming is an essential part of the Chinese cooking concept, since it is the Chinese theory that flavors are released and concentrated only if food materials are subjected—even though very shortly—to the high temperature of hot oil. The following few recipes illustrate how steaming is used in conjunction with stir-frying and the treatment of hot oil.

## STEAMED SQUASH WITH SHREDDED MUSHROOMS

Serves 5–6

1 large squash (about 3½ pounds)

4 medium-sized Chinese dried mushrooms
2–3 dried red chilies

1½ cups vegetarian stock
2 slices ginger root, finely
  shredded
1 teaspoon salt

pepper to taste
1 vegetarian stock cube
4 tablespoons vegetable oil
2 tablespoons soy sauce

Peel the squash if necessary and cut it into oblong pieces 3 by 1½ inches. Soak the mushrooms in hot water for half an hour, drain, remove and discard the stems, and cut the caps into shreds. Trim, seed, and shred the chilies.

Place the pieces of squash in a large, deep-sided, heatproof dish or Pyrex glass bowl. Add the stock and sprinkle with the shredded ginger, salt and pepper, and the crumbled stock cube. Insert the glass bowl or heatproof dish into a steamer and steam for half an hour. Stir and turn the contents over and steam for a further 15 minutes.

Meanwhile, heat the oil in a small pan or wok. When very hot, add the shredded chilies and mushrooms. Stir for 2–2½ minutes (the contents should be boiling). Remove the bowl or dish of squash from the steamer and pour away any excess liquid. Pour the chili oil and mushrooms evenly over the squash. Sprinkle with soy sauce and serve.

# STEAMED AND STIR-FRIED CARROTS AND TURNIPS

Serves 5–6

1 pound large carrots
1 pound white turnips
3 slices ginger root
½ cup vegetarian stock
½ teaspoon salt
pepper to taste

2 scallions
2 cloves garlic
3 tablespoons vegetable oil
2 tablespoons yellow bean
  sauce
1 tablespoon soy sauce

| 1 tablespoon hoisin sauce | 2 teaspoons sugar |
| 2 tablespoons red wine | 1½ tablespoons butter |

Scrape or peel the carrots and turnips and cut them slantwise into triangular pieces approximately 2½ by 2 inches. Shred the ginger. Place the vegetables and ginger in a heatproof dish. Add the stock, salt, and pepper. Insert the contents into a steamer and steam for half an hour.

Meanwhile, cut the scallions into ¼-inch shavings and coarsely chop the garlic. Heat the oil in a large frying pan. When hot, add the scallions, garlic, yellow bean sauce, soy sauce, hoisin sauce, red wine, and sugar and stir for 1 minute. Drain the carrots and turnips of any excess liquid. Pour the vegetables into the frying pan, add the butter, and stir-fry with the sauce ingredients in the pan over high heat for 2 minutes. Stir and turn until every piece of vegetable is well coated with sauce. Serve in a well-heated deep-sided dish, for the diners to consume with rice.

# STEAMED ASPARAGUS WITH EGG SAUCE

Serves 4–5

| 1½–2 pounds fresh asparagus | ½ vegetarian stock cube |
| EGG SAUCE: | 1 tablespoon cornstarch |
| 1 scallion | blended in 3 tablespoons |
| 2 Chinese salt eggs | water |
| 2 fresh eggs | 3 tablespoons butter |
| 1½ tablespoons vegetable oil | pepper to taste |
| ½ cup vegetarian stock | 2 tablespoons dry sherry |

Rinse the asparagus and remove the tougher end of the stems. Place the asparagus in a colander and insert them into a steamer. Steam vigorously for 25–30 minutes.

Coarsely chop the scallion and the salt eggs. Beat the fresh eggs lightly in a cup or bowl. Heat the oil in a small saucepan or wok. When hot, add the scallion and salt eggs. Stir for 1 minute over medium heat. Add the stock and crumbled stock cube and stir until the contents boil. Add the blended cornstarch and stir until the contents thicken. Remove the pan or wok from the heat. After a quarter of a minute, stir in the beaten eggs, butter, pepper, and sherry. Continue to stir until the mixture is consistent. Place the hot, freshly steamed asparagus on a well-heated serving dish, pour the sauce over them, and serve.

## STEAMED ZUCCHINI IN MUSHROOM SAUCE

Serves 4–5

4–5 medium-sized zucchini
(about 1½ pounds)

½ cup Mushroom Sauce (page 124)
1½ tablespoons butter

Clean and cut the zucchini slantwise into 1½-inch sections. Place them in a steamer and steam vigorously for 5–6 minutes.

Heat the mushroom sauce and butter in a saucepan or wok. When boiling, add the steamed zucchini. Stir and turn them for 2–3 minutes. Transfer to a well-heated serving dish and serve.

# STEAMED CAULIFLOWER IN BLACK
# BEAN AND TOMATO SAUCE

Serves 4–5

| | |
|---|---|
| 1 large cauliflower | ½ cup Tomato and Black |
| 1½ tablespoons butter | Bean Sauce (page 126) |

Trim most of the green leaves and the tougher parts of the stem from the cauliflower and cut it vertically into quarters. Place the four pieces of cauliflower in a colander, insert in a steamer, and steam vigorously for 18 minutes.

Heat the butter and sauce in a small saucepan or wok, stirring it a few times, until it boils.

Transfer the cauliflower to a well-heated serving dish, pour the boiling sauce over it, and serve.

# 4 RICE

Rice is the central point of all Chinese meals. The other dishes served, whether meat, poultry, fish, seafood, vegetables, or soup, and which may range from two or three to seven or eight, are all there to accompany and complement rice. A buffet of a dozen items may be served, including a whole fish, a large fowl, a knuckle of pork or a leg of lamb, a selection of soups, and stir-fried dishes, yet the meal is incomplete unless there is ample rice to complement them. The only time when rice is not served is at a formal banquet, when the dishes are served as courses, one after another, interspersed with wine drinking and toasting. As there are often a dozen courses or more, the Chinese banquet tends to be very lengthy and over-rich.

But the majority of people are much happier when there is ample rice to accompany the other dishes, and they much prefer to sit down to a good family dinner or an informal dinner party where rice is served to complement all the other dishes. After all, we are rice eaters; we need rice to cushion off the richness or spiciness of savory dishes. We enjoy the sensation of digging in to the rice to the accompaniment of a variety of foods and sauces, and washing them down with soup. Drinking and washing down rice and savory foods with soup is a sensation peculiar to the enjoyment of eating Chinese food. We Chinese do not drink water at mealtimes—least of all iced water!—nor do we absolutely require tea or wine, although we would sip at them if they are there, for there is always the provision of one or more soups, which are drunk continually throughout the meal. It is probably the diluting effect of soups and the ample amount of vegetables consumed, some in the soups themselves, which make most Chinese foods so easily digestible and comparatively healthy. Rice and vegetables are indeed the staple diet of the Chinese. Meat, fish, and seafood, like spices, are consumed only in small quantities as accompaniments to rice. In China when you ask a person whether he or she has eaten, you would say, "Have you had rice?"

Rice is cooked in two main ways in China: plain boiled or steamed. Both of these should be dry and flaky and are normally served at lunch and dinner. But at breakfast in China rice is usually eaten in the soft, porridgy form called soft rice, or congee (*chou* in Chinese).

These two basic rices can be further extended into numerous variations of fried rice, vegetable rice, topped rice, and savory soft rice (or congee) to suit people's palates and the time of the day.

Soft porridgy rice with no other added ingredients may seem oversimple, bland, and even insipid, but to connoisseurs it can be one of the most welcoming foods devised by man. Eaten at breakfast, it is very warming, cleansing, and refreshing, and to the invalid or semi-invalid it can be one of the most comforting and easily digestible of all foods. It is a pleasure to eat when accompanied by only a very small amount of pickles, salted or preserved eggs, or a few drops of good-quality soy sauce. Eating congee with these uncomplicated accompaniments while lying in bed is almost a part of the Chinese racial childhood memory.

Although cooking rice is simple, it should be done with great care.

## PLAIN BOILED RICE

It is easier to measure rice by volume than by weight. For ordinary *long-grain* rice the quantities are:

1 cup or small bowl of rice to 1¾ cup or bowl of water
   (enough for two)
2 cups or bowls of rice to 3 cups or bowls of water
3 cups or bowls of rice to 4¼ cups or bowls of water

With *oval-grain* rice, the percentage of water can be slightly reduced by a quarter cup or bowl per cup or bowl of rice to be cooked.

Rinse and drain the rice a couple of times. Add it to a heavy saucepan or casserole with a tight-fitting lid. Pour in the correct amount of water. Place the pan or casserole over medium heat and bring the contents to a boil. Boil for 3 minutes. Cover firmly and leave the contents to simmer over the lowest heat for 10 minutes. Turn the heat off altogether. Do not open the lid, but allow the rice to stand and continue to cook in the remaining heat for a further 10 minutes. By that time the rice should be ready to serve. Fluff it up with a wet spoon or chopsticks.

Cooked rice should keep warm easily for half an hour if not removed from the stove or placed in a drafty spot. If it does become cool it can easily be heated up by pouring in a few tablespoons of boiling water, turning on the heat underneath the pan for 1–2 minutes, and stirring.

## STEAMED RICE

Steaming is partly "wet-cooking," and since foods do not dry up as readily as when cooked or heated over a naked flame, approximately 20 percent less water is used than for boiled rice. Therefore, to steam 1 cup rice you add 1¼ cups water; for 2 cups rice you add 2½ cups water; and for 3 cups rice you add 4 cups water.

Rinse and drain the rice. Put the washed rice into a large or deep heatproof bowl or basin. Add the correct amount of water and leave the rice to soak for half an hour.

Place the bowl containing the rice on a rack in a large pan containing 2–3 inches of water: the water surface should not reach higher than 4 inches below the rim of the bowl. Cover the bowl and bring the water to a boil. Continue to simmer over gentle heat for 30 minutes, when the rice should be ready. Fluff the rice with a wet spoon or chopsticks and serve by bringing the bowl to the table, which should help to keep the rice hot.

Not infrequently in China rice is steamed in individual bowls and then brought to the table and served to each diner in the very bowl in which it has been cooked. In the winter the numerous steaming bowls of rice on the dining table present a very appealing and welcoming sight.

## BAKED RICE

In a modern Western kitchen rice can be baked very conveniently in an oven, if only to get it out of the way during cooking, when many other dishes need to be on the stove. It is probably best to use a casserole with a heavy lid, and the proportion of water used to cook with the rice should be in the same ratio as for boiled rice (page 106–7).

Preheat the oven to 400°F. Rinse and drain the rice. Put the rice and water, in the correct proportion, into a casserole. Bring the contents to a boil on the stove for 2–3 minutes. Cover the casserole, place in the oven, and bake for 12 minutes. Reduce the heat to 350°F and continue to bake for 12 minutes. The rice should be ready to serve. Fluff the rice with a wet spoon or a pair of wet chopsticks and bring the casserole to the table for the diners to serve themselves.

## BROWN RICE

Brown rice is becoming increasingly popular because of its nutritive qualities and the digestive value of the bran. Brown rice should be cooked in largely the same manner as ordinary white rice in the previous three recipes. The only difference is that nearly half as much water again is needed for the cooking, which should be continued at low heat for twice the length of time.

Rice cooked in these ways can be used for various forms of fried rice or vegetable rice, or served as a dish of topped rice, an economical and self-contained meal for one. Nowadays this is becoming a more and more popular way of eating in China, as people have become more mobile and cannot count on eating in large family or work groups any more.

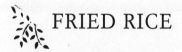 FRIED RICE

Almost any food that can be chopped small can be used for making fried rice.

## EGG FRIED RICE

One of the simplest and yet most popular fried rice dishes is egg fried rice. Simple as it is, this is a satisfying dish to eat even with only a very limited amount of accompaniments, such as some chopped pickles or just a tablespoon or two of soy sauce.

Serves 2–3, with at least one other dish

| | |
|---|---|
| 1 medium-sized onion | 2 scallions |
| 2 eggs | 3½ tablespoons vegetable oil |
| 1 teaspoon salt | 1½ bowls cold cooked rice |

Slice and coarsely chop the onion. Break the eggs into a cup, add the salt, and beat with a fork for 10 seconds. Trim and cut the scallions into fine shavings.

Heat the oil in a frying pan or wok. When hot, add the chopped onions and stir-fry in the hot oil for 45 seconds. Pour the beaten egg into one side of the pan or wok and add the rice on the other. When the eggs are about to set, scramble them, then bring them over and mix evenly with the rice that is being stir-fried in the same pan. Sprinkle with half the scallion shavings. Turn and stir the ingredients together.

Serve by transferring the contents to a large serving bowl or into individual bowls, and sprinkle the top of the fried rice with the remainder of the scallion shavings.

## VEGETABLE FRIED RICE

Almost any kind of vegetable can be chopped, stir-fried, and mixed into the fried rice. Favorite ingredients are mushrooms and chopped pickles. Fried rice cooked with several ingredients can be eaten with satisfaction even without other accompaniments. It is most suitable to prepare when there is a lot of leftover food lying about. Serve in a large common serving bowl, or in 3–4 individual bowls. Sprinkle the fried rice in the bowls with chopped scallions and 1½ tablespoons soy sauce.

Serves 2–3, or serve with 1 or 2 other dishes

| | |
|---|---|
| 1 medium-sized onion | 1½ teaspoons salt |
| 1 medium-sized young carrot | 5 tablespoons vegetable oil |
| 1 medium-sized pepper | 3–4 tablespoons green peas |
| 2 medium-sized tomatoes | 3 ounces bean sprouts |
| 2 scallions | 2 bowls cooked rice |
| 2 eggs | 1¼ tablespoons soy sauce |

Cut the onion into thin slices. Clean and chop the carrot and pepper into ¼-inch cubes. Cut the tomato into ½-inch slices and then into ¼-inch pieces. Cut the scallions into ¼-inch shavings. Beat the eggs with half the salt.

Heat 4 tablespoons of the oil in a large frying pan or wok. When hot, add the onion and carrot. Stir and turn in the hot oil for 1 minute. Add the pepper, tomatoes, peas, bean sprouts, and salt. Stir them all together for one minute and push to one side of the pan or wok. Add the remaining oil to the other side of the pan. When hot, pour in the beaten egg. Add the rice to the vegetable side of the pan or wok and spread it evenly over the vegetables. When the eggs are set, scramble them, then bring them over to mix and turn with the vegetables and rice. Continue to stir and turn until the ingredients are evenly mixed. Transfer to a large bowl or basin, sprinkle the top with soy sauce, and serve.

# VEGETABLE RICE

Vegetable rice differs from fried rice in that it is cooked while the rice is cooking itself. It is possibly less refined than fried rice and very much a dish of the masses. It should really be eaten with at least one other dish.

111

# VEGETABLE RICE WITH EGGPLANT, CARROT, ONION, AND CABBAGE

This should be cooked during the preparation of 2–3 cups or bowls of boiled rice or baked rice. One of the attractions of the dish is that much of the flavor and quality of the vegetables will have permeated the surrounding rice. Rice and vegetables cooked this way are best served and eaten with at least one stir-fried dish.

Serves 4–5, with at least one other dish

| | |
|---|---|
| ½ medium-sized eggplant | 4 ounces cabbage |
| 1 medium-sized carrot | 3½ tablespoons vegetable oil |
| 1 medium-sized onion | 1 teaspoon salt |

Wash and clean all the vegetables. Cut the eggplant into 1-inch wedges, roll-cut the carrot into sections ½ inch thick, and chop the onion and cabbage into thin slices. Heat the oil in a frying pan or wok. When hot, add the carrot and eggplant and stir-fry over medium heat for 1½ minutes. Add the salt, onion, and cabbage and stir and turn together for a further 1 minute.

While cooking the boiled rice (when the rice has boiled for 3 minutes and simmered for 10 minutes) or baked rice (when the rice has boiled for 3 minutes and baked for 10 minutes), most of the moisture will have evaporated. Make a hole in the middle of the rice and put the partially cooked stir-fried ingredients into it together with the oil and juices from the pan. Cover the vegetables with the surrounding rice and return the saucepan to cook gently for a further 10 minutes, or for the casserole to bake, covered, for a further 12 minutes. Without removing the lid, allow the contents to stand and cook in the remaining heat for a further 5 minutes. The dish should now be ready to serve.

# VEGETABLE RICE WITH MUSHROOMS, ONIONS, TOMATOES, AND BROCCOLI

This should be cooked during the preparation of steamed rice. As with the previous recipe for vegetable rice, it is best to eat the dish with a stir-fried dish. A stir-fried dish cooked quickly over high heat has a greater intensity of flavor than a dish that has been cooked largely through steaming, where the flavor has been more lengthily dispersed throughout the whole dish during the process of cooking. It is a matter of balancing a bulk food dish, which is only lightly flavored, with a dish where the flavor is more concentrated as a result of the way in which it was cooked.

Serves 4–5, with at least one stir-fried dish

| | |
|---|---|
| 1 medium-sized onion | 2 cloves garlic |
| 4 ounces button mushrooms | 3½ tablespoons vegetable oil |
| 2–3 medium-sized tomatoes | 1½ teaspoons salt |
| 4 ounces broccoli | |

Cut the onion into thin slices. Cut each mushroom into halves or quarters, and the tomatoes into quarters and each segment into halves. Cut or break the broccoli into florets or ½-inch slices. Crush and chop the garlic.

Heat the oil in a frying pan or wok. When hot, add the onion, broccoli, and garlic. Stir-fry over medium heat for 1½ minutes. Add the mushrooms and salt and stir-fry for another minute. Add the tomato and continue stir-frying for 1 more minute.

While in the process of cooking steamed rice, and after the rice has been steamed for 20 minutes, make a hole in the middle and transfer the contents of the frying pan into the hole in the rice. Cover it with the surrounding rice and return the basin to steam, covered, for a further 12 minutes. The vegetable rice should now be ready to serve.

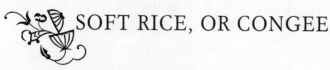 # SOFT RICE, OR CONGEE

Porridgy soft rice is a Chinese institution, a taste for which can only be acquired through having it for breakfast for some seasons. Its appeal and character lie in its being warm, comforting, and refreshing, and these qualities are enhanced when quantities of the rice are eaten with small amounts of strong-tasting, spicy, salted, smoked, pickled, preserved, and sometimes aromatic foods (such as roasted salted peanuts). What is attractive about soft rice is emphatically not its savoriness or tastiness but its total lack of either; perhaps it is this invariability (like that of porridge) which makes us feel it is one of the cornerstones of life. It therefore deserves to be cooked with care.

## PLAIN SOFT RICE, OR CONGEE

The hot pot or pan of soft rice is often brought to the table or placed on a side table for people to help themselves from at breakfast time. Soft rice is also served for midnight suppers (after lengthy mahjong games, for example). Because of the high heat content of congee, cold leftover savory dishes are often brought out from the pantry and served with hot congee without needing to be reheated.

Serves 5–6, with a small amount of highly seasoned foods

6–7 ounces long-grain rice
6–7 ounces oval-grain ice

3–4 ounces glutinous rice
 (short, round grains)
8–10 cups water

Rinse, wash, and drain the rice a couple of times. Add it to a large deep saucepan with the water. Bring to a boil, stir, and simmer over gentle heat for 30 minutes. Partially cover the saucepan and reduce the heat to very low. Continue to simmer slowly for 1½ hours, stirring now and then. At the end of that time the rice will have absorbed all the water and become a white, consistent gruel. It will keep hot or warm for a long time, but even if it is allowed to get cool or cold it can be readily reheated. Unlike Scottish porridge, a supply of congee for breakfast can be cooked for two or more days.

# SAVORY VEGETABLE SOFT RICE, OR SAVORY CONGEE

In contrast to plain soft rice or congee, savory congee has unlimited variations. In nonvegetarian cooking there are such famous savory congees as sampan congee (with seafood), the Cantonese chicken congee, or the Nanking pressed duck congee. Even in vegetarian cooking, where the number of ingredients used is necessarily limited, the range is considerable. The aim is to produce a soft rice that is only mildly but generally savory. Whichever vegetables are cooked in it, the length of cooking time allows the flavor to blend into the rice. But its appeal is highlighted by the small bits of highly seasoned foods (such as salted, pickled, and marinated foods) that are dispersed and embedded in the soft rice. These will only have been cooked for a short time, and the flavors will not yet have spread to the rice. The same effect is produced when a large dollop or two of highly seasoned or savory sauces (see pages 123–28) are poured on top of the soft rice just before serving. The same sauces are equally good with flaky, plain boiled rice served as topped rice; that is, without the usual accompaniment of several savory dishes.

# SAVORY VEGETABLE SOFT RICE WITH CABBAGE, PICKLE, AND BEAN SPROUTS

Serve hot, and let people help themselves from the cooking pot. As savory soft rice is an informal snack, no formality should be observed in its eating and serving. Most people are expected to help themselves to more than one helping.

Serves 4–5

12 ounces heart of Chinese or savoy cabbage
3 tablespoons vegetable oil
1 teaspoon salt
4–5 cups cooked soft rice

1½ vegetarian stock cubes
3–4 ounces bean sprouts
2½ tablespoons chopped snow pickle

Wash and cut the cabbage heart into 2-by-1-by-1½-inch pieces. Heat the oil in a large heavy saucepan. When hot, add the salt and cabbage and stir-fry for 2 minutes. Pour in the soft rice and add the crumbled stock cubes and ½ cup water. Stir them together so that the ingredients are evenly distributed. Continue to cook and simmer gently over very low heat for 1 hour, until the cabbage has become so soft that it almost becomes part of the rice. Sprinkle with the bean sprouts and chopped pickle. Stir a few times, cook for a further 4–5 minutes, and serve.

# SAVORY VEGETABLE SOFT RICE WITH BROCCOLI OR ASPARAGUS STEMS, CARROTS, PICKLE, AND SALTED DUCK EGGS

Serves 4–5

12 ounces broccoli or asparagus stems
2 medium-sized carrots
2–3 salted duck eggs (page 53)
2 scallions

3 tablespoons vegetable oil
1 teaspoon salt
1½ vegetarian stock cubes
4–5 cups cooked soft rice
1½ tablespoons chopped snow pickle

Cut the broccoli or asparagus stems into 1½-by-½-inch pieces. Clean and cut the carrots slantwise into ½-inch slices. Chop the duck eggs into ¼-inch pieces. Cut the scallions into ¼-inch shavings, separating the white parts from the green.

Heat the oil in a heavy saucepan or casserole. When hot, add the broccoli or asparagus, carrots, and salt, and stir-fry for 2 minutes. Add ½ cup water and the crumbled stock cubes and pour in the soft rice. Stir until the ingredients are evenly distributed. Continue to cook and simmer gently over very low heat for 1 hour, until the vegetables are well cooked and have almost become part of the soft rice. Add half the chopped salted egg, the snow pickle, and the whites of the scallions. Stir a few times and cook gently for a further 4–5 minutes. Sprinkle the top of the soft rice with the remainder of the chopped duck eggs and the scallion greens. Serve hot, as above.

# SAVORY VEGETABLE SOFT RICE WITH DRIED AND FRESH MUSHROOMS, SALTED KELP, BRAISED BAMBOO SHOOTS, CHOPPED WATERCRESS, AND SOY-BRAISED EGGS

Serves 4–5

5–6 medium-sized Chinese dried mushrooms
8 ounces fresh button mushrooms
3–4 ounces braised bamboo shoots (available canned)
3–4 ounces kelp

3 soy-braised eggs
3–4 pounds watercress leaves
3 tablespoons vegetable oil
½ teaspoon salt
1½ vegetarian stock cubes
4–5 cups cooked soft rice

Soak the dried mushrooms in ½ cup hot water for half an hour and drain, reserving the water. Discard the mushroom stems and cut each cap into quarters. Cut each button mushroom into ½-inch slices, and cut the braised bamboo shoots into 1½-inch sections. Wash the kelp and cut into similar-sized pieces. Cut the soy eggs into ¼-inch pieces. Coarsely chop the watercress leaves.

Heat the oil in a large saucepan or casserole. When hot, add the dried mushrooms, kelp, and braised bamboo shoots. Stir-fry for 2 minutes. Add the fresh mushrooms and salt and continue to stir-fry for 2 minutes. Pour in the mushroom water, the crumbled stock cubes, and the soft rice. Stir and turn the contents together so that they are evenly distributed. Continue to cook and simmer gently for 1 hour, until the vegetables have softened and almost become part of the soft rice. Sprinkle with half the chopped watercress leaves and the soy eggs. Stir a few times and continue to cook gently for a further 4–5 minutes.

Sprinkle the top of the soft rice with the remainder of the chopped watercress leaves and soy eggs just before serving. Serve hot, as above.

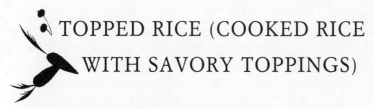

# TOPPED RICE (COOKED RICE WITH SAVORY TOPPINGS)

Topped rice reflects the changing scene of Chinese eating. In the past, and even on the majority of occasions today, a Chinese meal would be a communal affair where people dine together (whether family, friends, or workmates) and the dishes are shared by all those at the table. It is rather like having a sit-down hot buffet, where each diner brings only his or her bowl of rice and partakes of all the savory dishes served on the table. The Chinese, whether abroad or at home, have become more and more mobile, so they find themselves dining on their own much more frequently. On these occasions he or she will have the meal served in individual portions rather than from dishes as part of a large buffet spread, where the diners can simply help themselves.

To meet the requirements of the average Chinese, the best way to serve an essentially Chinese meal in individual portions is to have rice served as a bed in a large bowl or a deep-sided dish, and to have it topped with a miniature dish or two (a case of Chinese *cuisine minceur*), where preferably at least one dish should have a sauce (to provide the "gravy")—and if there are two dishes served they should, if possible, be prepared from contrasting ingredients and one should be crunchy. And in the combination, if one dish is rich and spicy, the other should have a lighter, fresher, and more natural flavor. On the other hand, one might be limited to a single dish for an individual portion, in which case one should choose a dish that combines both the rich and spicy foods and the lighter, fresher, more natural-tasting ones.

Luckily, scores of Chinese dishes are qualified to fulfill these guidelines. If you scan the dishes contained in the section on stir-fried vegetable dishes (pages 69–79), you will notice that there are at least a dozen dishes that are appropriate. If they do not entirely fulfill these

119

requirements, I recommend that you use the foods from two different dishes as garnish or full-portion toppings on rice so that you have several portions of composite topped-rice dishes (or meals): say, for example, a simple, light-tasting dish of Stir-fried Young Cabbage with Ginger and Snow Pickles (page 74) with the much spicier Sichuan Hot-braised Stir-fried Eggplant (page 88); or the comparatively dry Four Soy-braised Chunky Vegetables with Pickles (page 87) can be used in conjunction with the more soupy Stir-fried Semi-soup Dish of Mushrooms, Pickles, Braised Bamboo Shoots, Broccoli, Transparent Noodles, and Seaweed (page 95).

The appeal of these miniature, topped-rice, "self-contained" meals is readily enhanced by Chinese relishes—homemade pickles, soy-marinated and salted vegetables—and savory vegetable sauces, although these are only used in small quantities.

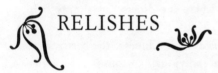

# RELISHES

## HOMEMADE PICKLES

These are generally made from any three, four, or five of the following vegetables:

cucumbers, carrots,
radishes, turnips
white cabbage (Chinese or savoy)

celery, onions
leeks, green beans
green peppers, red peppers
scallions, ginger root

Pickles are usually made in thoroughly cleaned, airtight glazed earthen or glass jars. For 1–1½ quarts you will need 6–8 cups cold boiled water, 1¼ tablespoons salt, 3–4 chili peppers, 2 teaspoons Sichuan peppercorns (lightly pounded), 1½ tablespoons sugar, 5–6 slices ginger root, and 2 tablespoons white rum, gin, or vodka. The vegetables should be thoroughly cleaned, trimmed, and peeled (if preferred), then well drained and cut into large pieces.

Pour the cold boiled water into the jar. First add the salt, chilies, peppercorns, ginger, liquor, and sugar, followed by the selected vegetables. Firmly screw or press on the top of the jar and see that it is airtight. Place the jar in a cool place and let it stand for a week before using. The longer the wait, the better the pickles.

The vegetables can be extracted from the jar with a very clean pair of chopsticks, or with tongs, but do not allow any grease to enter the jar. When serving a topped-rice dish, the pickled vegetable may be cut into smaller slices and placed in small quantities of about 1½–2 tablespoons at the edge of the rice.

## HOMEMADE SALTED VEGETABLES

Mustard greens, turnip leaves, and collard greens are most generally used. The usual process is to place a heap of vegetables on greaseproof paper and leave for three days, turning and reheaping at the end of each day to allow them to age and mature.

After three days, cut the vegetables into lengthwise strips, rinse them in cold water, and dry them thoroughly. To ensure that they are thoroughly dried, spread them out to air in a breezy spot for 4–5 hours.

Place the vegetables in a wide-mouth jar in layers 1 inch thick, sprinkling the top of each layer with 1½–2 teaspoons of salt. Repeat this process until you have almost reached the top of the jar. Place a smaller jar inside the wide-mouth jar, and a weight on top of the smaller jar to press down the salting vegetables inside. Leave the vegetables for two days. Turn the vegetables over, and pack them again under pressure for two more days, pouring any accumulated liquid over them. Repeat once more, and after approximately a week's salting the vegetables will be ready for use. They will keep in a refrigerator almost indefinitely.

To use, cut the salted vegetables into ¼–½-inch pieces and pile them in small heaps by the edge of the rice to be savored as a "side item" along with pickles.

## HOMEMADE SOY-MARINATED VEGETABLES

Soy-marinated vegetables are yet another form of relish that is consumed extensively in China to augment the variety of flavors to be enjoyed in a Chinese meal. They can be included even in a miniature meal, such as that of a self-contained dish of topped rice.

The vegetables most frequently used are white turnips, carrots, beets, cucumber, and green kohlrabi.

Wash the vegetables and dry them well. Cut them lengthwise into julienne strips. Place the vegetables in a quart jar until about three-quarters full and add 1 teaspoon salt and 1½ tablespoons sugar. Shake well so that each piece of vegetable is coated. Leave to stand overnight.

Add enough good-quality soy sauce to just cover the vegetables. As in the case of salted vegetables, use a smaller jar that will fit inside the wide-mouth jar to press down the vegetables, so that all the vegetables are submerged and the air bubbles expelled. After marinating overnight, the soy-marinated vegetables are ready to use as a relish, in the same manner as the salted vegetables and pickles. If you like, 2–3 teaspoons of chili sauce or red chili oil may be added to the marinade to slightly pep up the spiciness of the relish.

## SOY-MARINATED SHREDDED GINGER

Since ginger is used extensively in Chinese food and cooking, it is often preserved in shredded form so that it may be produced at a moment's notice. Shredded ginger is also often used as a relish or side item, on a dish of fried rice or topped rice, for those who like its sharp flavor. Since marinated ginger root contained in a jar keeps for months, it can be made in any quantity to suit your need.

Wash and thoroughly dry the ginger root. Use a paring knife to scrape off the skin. Wipe and dry each piece with absorbent paper. Use a sharp knife to cut each piece into paper-thin slices, and then further cut into fine shreds, about 1–1½ inches long. Place them in an airtight jar and pour in enough light soy sauce to cover (add 1 or 2 shredded dried chili peppers if you wish). Let stand overnight. The shredded ginger is then ready for use.

# SAVORY VEGETABLE SAUCES

There are a number of savory vegetable sauces that can be added to rice (whether plain, fried, or topped) with beneficial results. They are normally added in quantities of no more than 2–3 tablespoonfuls. On top of the rice, they occupy a place between the larger quantities of topped foods (which make up between a quarter and a third of the actual dish) and the relishes (pickles, salted and marinated vegetables) which are only provided in quantities of a tablespoon or two. Yet their contribution to a dish of rice can be quite significant. Most of these sauces have a fairly concentrated flavor. Their presence in a topped-rice dish paves the way between the sharp flavor of the relishes and the more general savory flavor and quantity of topped foods.

When all three of these are present, a dish of topped rice can often be as appealing and satisfying as a complete, multi-dish Chinese meal.

## MUSHROOM SAUCE

This savory sauce should be added in quantities of 2–4 tablespoons to a portion of rice as one of the constituents of a dish of topped rice.

Serves 4–5

8 ounces mushrooms
6 medium-sized Chinese dried
  mushrooms
2 scallions
1½ tablespoons vegetable oil
1½ tablespoons Sichuan Ja
  Tsai pickle, finely chopped
½ tablespoon yellow bean
  sauce
1 tablespoon soy sauce

½ tablespoon hoisin sauce
½ cup vegetarian stock
1 vegetarian stock cube
¼ teaspoon salt
1½ tablespoons butter or
  margarine
1 teaspoon sesame oil
2½ teaspoons cornstarch
  blended in 2 tablespoons
  water

Clean the mushrooms and cut them into thin slices. Soak the dried mushrooms in hot water for half an hour, drain, remove and discard the stems, and cut the caps into shreds. Cut the scallions into ¼-inch shavings, separating the whites from the greens.

Heat the oil in a saucepan or wok. When hot, add the dried mushrooms, the pickle, and the whites of the scallions. Stir for 1½ minutes. Add the mushrooms and continue to stir and turn for 1½ minutes. Add the yellow bean sauce, soy sauce, and hoisin sauce and stir for 2 minutes. Pour in the vegetarian stock and add the crumbled vegetarian stock cube, salt, and butter or margarine. Cook over low heat for 5–6 minutes. Add the scallion greens and sesame oil. Stir and turn for 1 minute. Add the blended cornstarch. Stir until the sauce thickens.

# SICHUAN EGGPLANT AND BAMBOO SHOOT SAUCE

Use this sauce in the same manner and quantity as in the previous recipe.

Serves 4–5

1 medium-sized eggplant
4 ounces marinated bamboo
  shoots (available canned)
1–2 dried chilies (to taste)
1–2 fresh chilies (to taste)
2 slices ginger root
2½ tablespoons vegetable oil
½ teaspoon salt
¾ cup vegetarian stock

1 vegetarian stock cube
½ tablespoon light soy sauce
1½ tablespoons butter or
  margarine
1 teaspoon sesame oil
2½ teaspoons cornstarch
  blended in 2 tablespoons
  water

Remove the ends of the eggplant (including the stem) and cut into pieces the size of quarter of a sugar lump. Cut the marinated bamboo shoots into pieces the same size. Trim and seed the chilies and finely chop them. Finely chop the ginger, too.

Heat the oil in a saucepan or wok. When hot, add the chilies and ginger and stir-fry for 1 minute. Add the bamboo shoots, salt, and eggplant. Stir and turn over high heat for 2 minutes. Pour in the stock and add the crumbled stock cube and soy sauce. When the contents boil, stir and cook the ingredients together over low heat for 10 minutes. Add the butter or margarine and sesame oil and continue to stir and turn for 1 minute. Add the cornstarch mixture and stir until the sauce thickens.

## TOMATO AND BLACK BEAN SAUCE

Use and serve in the same manner and quantity as the sauces in the two previous recipes.

Serves 4–5

5–6 medium-sized tomatoes
1 tablespoon salted black
   beans
2 medium-sized zucchini
1 medium-sized onion
4 cloves garlic
3 tablespoons vegetable oil
½ teaspoon salt
½ cup vegetarian stock
2 teaspoons sugar
3 tablespoons dry sherry

1 pinch pepper
4 tablespoons tomato paste
1 vegetarian stock cube
1 tablespoon light soy sauce
½ tablespoon dark soy sauce
1½ tablespoons butter
1 teaspoon sesame oil
2½ teaspoons cornstarch
   blended in 2 tablespoons
   water

Cut the tomatoes into sugar-lump-sized pieces. Soak the black beans for 5 minutes, drain, and mash. Trim the zucchini and cut them into pieces half as big as the tomato pieces. Cut the onion into very thin slices. Crush and coarsely chop the garlic.

Heat the oil in a saucepan or wok. When hot, add the onion and stir for 1 minute. Add the garlic, black beans, and salt and continue to stir for half a minute. Add the zucchini and tomatoes and stir and turn them all together over high heat for 3 minutes.

Add the stock, sugar, sherry, pepper, tomato purée, and crumbled stock cube. Bring to a boil, reduce the heat, and simmer for 7–8 minutes, stirring now and then. Add soy sauce, butter, and sesame oil. Stir and cook for 1 more minute. Finally, add the blended cornstarch. Stir until the sauce thickens.

## EGG SAUCE WITH MASHED LIMA BEANS AND SCALLIONS

Serve and use in the same manner and quantity as the sauces in the previous recipes.

Serves 4–5

4 eggs
2 scallions
2 cloves garlic
2 tablespoons snow pickle
6 ounces lima beans
3 tablespoons vegetable oil
¾ cup vegetarian stock
1 teaspoon salt
1½ teaspoons sugar

2 tablespoons dry sherry
1 vegetarian stock cube
2 tablespoons butter or margarine
1 tablespoon light soy sauce
2½ teaspoons cornstarch blended in 2 tablespoons water
1 teaspoon sesame oil

Beat the eggs lightly for 10 seconds with a fork. Cut the scallions into ¼-inch shavings, separating the whites from the greens. Coarsely crush and chop the garlic and pickle and mix together with the whites of the scallions. Boil the lima beans for 30–45 minutes, or until soft, then drain and mash them.

Heat the oil in a saucepan or wok. When hot, add the scallion whites, garlic, and pickle and stir them in the hot oil for 1½ minutes. Add the stock and salt, mashed lima beans, sugar, sherry, and crumbled stock cube. Stir until the contents are well integrated. Bring to a boil, reduce to a simmer, and cook gently over low heat for 7–8 minutes. Stir in the beaten eggs. Stir until the eggs set and the contents have become smooth and consistent. Add the butter or margarine and the soy sauce, stir, and cook for a further half minute. Add the cornstarch mixture and stir until the sauce thickens. Sprinkle with the sesame oil.

# 5 SOUPS

Soup in China is a much more integral part of a meal than in the West. It does not stand alone at the beginning of a meal, to be eaten separately, but is eaten throughout the meal between mouthfuls of other foods. It is meant to complement the other foods rather than to lend more weight to the meal, and in contrast to the other dishes served on the table, which are mostly solids, the average Chinese soups are mostly clear. Large chunks of solid foods, clearly seen suspended in the transparent soup, add flavor to the meal and are picked out with chopsticks to be eaten separately, but the soups themselves are drunk as clear hot drinks to accompany rice and other solid dishes on the table. However, this does not mean that there are no thick soups in the Chinese repertoire. Indeed many well-known Chinese soups, such as hot and sour soup, shark's fin soup, and West Lake minced beef soup, are thick soups, but they are not served very often. Since soups are not meant to lend weight to a meal, it is not customary in Chinese cooking automatically to grind food to a pulp and use this as a basic ingredient for porridgy soup, which is the tendency in Western cooking.

We Chinese are very particular about flavor: a soup may be clear, but it must be flavorful. A distinctive flavor can be created from a combination of ingredients, or from using a quantity of one single ingredient, or from the flavor of the original broth. In order to achieve a clear broth, which is usually required to make a Chinese soup, the ordinary vegetarian stock, based on slow-cooked beans (page 30), will need to be strained two or three times. Water is often used instead of stock or broth, since the latter both require such a considerable time to become absolutely clear. Chunkily cut, hard vegetables are simmered for a period of time and then a small quantity of ingredients such as vegetable concentrates or seasonings are added to pep up the flavor. Leaf vegetables are normally added only a very few minutes before the soup is ready, to provide both a freshening effect as well as an additional flavor.

Generally in Chinese vegetarian cooking the hard stems or roots of vegetables are cooked in the soup to provide the long-term flavoring, and the leaf vegetables are cooked for just a short time to provide a fresh dimension, with the seasonings, sauces, or flavoring agents only being included to complement the bulk flavor of the dish and to provide that added zest. Since the main bulk food eaten in a Chinese meal is rice, which is meant to be plain, neutral, and bland, it generally requires a tasty soup to complement it.

We shall start with a few simple soups, and the simplest of all is Egg Drop Soup.

## EGG DROP SOUP

This is often seen on Chinese dinner tables, whether at home or in offices, canteens, or student dining rooms. It can be produced in 2–3 minutes. The soup should be served in a large bowl for the diners to help themselves from during the course of the meal.

Serves 4–5

| | |
|---|---|
| 1 or 2 eggs | 1½ teaspoons salt |
| 2 scallions | pepper to taste |

2½–3 cups boiling water           1 vegetarian stock cube
1 cup vegetarian stock

Beat the egg for 10 seconds with a fork or chopsticks. Coarsely chop the scallions, separating the whites from the greens.

Add the scallion whites, salt, and pepper to a saucepan or wok. Pour in the boiling water. When the contents have boiled, pour in the beaten egg very slowly along the prongs of a fork, twirling evenly over the surface of the soup. Sprinkle the scallion greens into the soup. Add the vegetarian stock and crumbled stock cube. Bring to the boil, stir, and serve.

## EGG DROP SOUP WITH TOMATOES

### Serves 4–5

Repeat the previous recipe, using 3–4 medium-sized tomatoes. Cut the tomatoes into segments and add them to the soup with the whites of the scallions. Then proceed in the same manner as in the previous recipe. Adjust the seasonings toward the end, as the tomatoes will increase the volume of the soup.

## SPINACH AND BRAISED BAMBOO SHOOT SOUP

Serve in a large soup bowl for the diners to help themselves from during the meal. Very often a cake of bean curd is cut into sugar-lump-sized cubes and added to the soup for a minute's cooking before serving.

Serves 4–5

1 pound fresh spinach
4 ounces braised bamboo
    shoots (available canned)
3½ tablespoons vegetable oil
1 teaspoon salt
2 teaspoons sugar
1 quart water

1 vegetarian stock cube
1 tablespoon light soy sauce
1 tablespoon cornstarch
    blended in 3 tablespoons
    water
1 teaspoon sesame oil

Wash and thoroughly drain the spinach. Remove tough stems and discolored leaves. Cut the braised bamboo shoots into 2-by-¼-inch thin strips.

Heat 2½ tablespoons of the oil in a large pan or wok. When hot, add half the spinach. When this has wilted, add the second half with the remaining oil. Sprinkle the spinach evenly with salt and sugar. After 1 minute, remove the spinach and pour away any extracted water.

Heat the quart of water in the pan or wok. When it boils, add the bamboo shoots, crumbled stock cube, and soy sauce. Allow the contents to simmer together for 1½ minutes. Return the spinach to the pan or wok. Stir the contents so that the ingredients are evenly distributed in the soup. Adjust the seasonings, then add the blended cornstarch. When the contents return to a boil, sprinkle the soup with sesame oil.

## BEAN SPROUT AND SOYBEAN SOUP

Serve in a large soup bowl for the diners to help themselves from during the meal. This is a fairly substantial soup, which should add to the bulk and nourishment of a meal.

Serves 4–5

| | |
|---|---|
| 12 ounces bean sprouts | 2 cups vegetarian stock |
| 6 ounces soybeans | ½ teaspoon sugar |
| 1 quart water | 1 vegetarian stock cube |
| ½ teaspoon salt | 1 tablespoon light soy sauce |
| 2 scallions | 1 teaspoon sesame oil |
| 3 tablespoons vegetable oil | |

Wash and shake the bean sprouts in water, drain, and set aside. Rinse the beans and bring to a boil in 2 cups of the water with the salt. Simmer gently for 1 hour until the beans are quite soft. Coarsely chop the scallions.

Heat the oil in a large pan or wok. When hot, add the sprouts and stir-fry for 2 minutes. Pour the cooked beans and the stock into the pan. Add the sugar and the remaining 2 cups water. When the contents return to a boil, sprinkle the soup with the crumbled stock cube and the soy sauce. Stir and simmer for 2 minutes. Sprinkle with the chopped scallions and sesame oil and serve.

## CREAM OF SPINACH (OR GREEN CABBAGE) SOUP, OR GREEN JADE SOUP

This is another fairly substantial soup which should add to the bulk and nourishment of the meal. Its green color should particularly appeal to the Western palate, which is used to soups of this type.

Serves 4–5

10 ounces young spinach
1 tablespoon Sichuan Ja Tsai
  pickle
1 cake bean curd
2 cloves garlic
3 tablespoons vegetable oil
1 teaspoon salt
2 cups water
2 cups vegetarian stock

1 vegetarian stock cube
1½ tablespoons light soy
  sauce
1½ tablespoons butter or
  margarine
1½ tablespoons cornstarch
  blended in 3 tablespoons
  water

Rinse the spinach and remove tough stems and discolored leaves. Place half the spinach in a blender or food processor with half the pickle and purée. Repeat with the remaining spinach and pickle. Cut the bean curd into ¼-inch cubes (or smaller). Coarsely crush and chop the garlic.

Heat the oil in a saucepan or wok. When hot, add the puréed spinach and pickle, the garlic, and the salt. Stir-fry over medium heat for 2 minutes. Pour in the water and stir. When contents boil, add the stock and the crumbled stock cube. Bring back to a boil and add the chopped bean curd and soy sauce. Allow the contents to simmer together for a further 2 minutes. Adjust the seasonings. Add the butter or margarine and blended cornstarch. Turn and stir a few times and serve.

## CREAM OF CORN SOUP WITH GREEN PEAS, CARROTS, AND PEPPERS

A very quick and easy soup to make—yet a substantial and satisfying one.

Serves 4–5

2 tablespoons vegetable oil
1 teaspoon salt
2–4 ounces diced frozen peas, carrots, and red peppers
6–8 ounces canned cream of corn

2 cups water
1 cup vegetarian stock
1 vegetarian stock cube
1 tablespoon butter
salt and pepper to taste

Heat the oil in a saucepan or wok. When hot, add the salt and the frozen vegetables and stir together for half a minute. Pour in the corn and water. When the contents come to a boil, add the stock, sprinkle with the crumbled stock cube, and gently simmer for 5–6 minutes. Adjust the seasonings, stir in the butter, and serve.

## CHINESE WHITE CABBAGE SOUP

Every winter there seems to be a superabundant crop of white cabbage in northern China. Because of the quantity of the cabbage used to make this soup, it is full of flavor, and consequently it is one of the most widely served soups in China for half the year. It is even served for breakfast sometimes. Although a clear soup, it is often spooned into the diner's rice bowl, and the cabbage and rice are eaten together with great satisfaction.

Serves 4–5

1 medium-sized Chinese white Tientsin cabbage (2–3 pounds)
2 dried red chilies
2 tablespoons snow pickle
3–4 Chinese dried mushrooms

3 tablespoons vegetable oil
1 teaspoon salt
1 quart water
1 vegetarian stock cube
salt and pepper to taste

Wash and cut the cabbage into 2-inch sections. Trim and seed the chilies and cut them and the pickle into thin shreds. Soak the dried mushrooms in hot water for half an hour, remove and discard the stems, and cut the caps into similar thin shreds.

Heat the oil in a saucepan or wok. When hot, add the salt, pickle, chilies, and mushrooms. Stir over medium heat for 1½ minutes. Add the cabbage and continue to stir and turn for 2 minutes. Pour in the water and sprinkle with the crumbled stock cube. Bring to a boil and simmer for 10 minutes. Adjust the seasonings and serve.

## WHITE TURNIP SOUP

There are other Chinese vegetable soups where quality and character are derived from the weight and quantity of the vegetable used. They are simple, unfanciful soups with plenty of personality. The large quantity of turnips gives the character to this soup. After a comparatively lengthy cooking, the vegetable becomes tender and very appealing when consumed in large chunky pieces, to be eaten with rice and washed down with mouthfuls of soup.

Serves 4–5

| | |
|---|---|
| 1½ pounds white turnips | 3 cups water |
| 1½ tablespoons snow pickle | 2 cups double-strained vege- |
| 1½ tablespoons Sichuan Ja | tarian stock |
| Tsai pickle | ½ teaspoon sugar |
| 2½ tablespoons vegetable oil | 1 vegetarian stock cube |
| 1 teaspoon salt | salt and pepper to taste |

Peel the turnips and cut them into 1½-by-1-inch wedges. Coarsely chop the pickles. Heat the oil in a saucepan or wok. When hot, add the pickles and stir-fry for 1 minute. Add the turnips, salt, and water. Bring to a boil. Reduce heat and simmer gently for 40 minutes. Add the stock, sugar, and crumbled stock cube. Turn contents over a few times. Adjust the seasonings, cook gently for 5 more minutes, and serve.

## CARROT AND CUCUMBER SOUP

Once again, because of the large quantity of carrots and cucumber, the soup is full of vegetable flavor. For the rice eater it is an enjoyable soup to drink and eat not only because of the richness of the soup but also because of the vegetables, which can be eaten with mouthfuls of rice.

Serves 4–5

1½ pounds large young carrots
8 ounces cucumber
2 scallions
1½ tablespoons snow pickle
2½ tablespoons vegetable oil
4 slices ginger root

1 teaspoon salt
3 cups water
2 cups double-strained vegetarian stock
1 vegetarian stock cube
salt and pepper to taste

Scrape or peel the carrots and cut slantwise into ½-inch slices. Cut the unpeeled cucumber into 1-inch wedges, and the scallions into ¼-inch shavings, separating the whites from the greens. Chop the pickles into small pieces.

Heat the oil in a saucepan or wok. When hot, add the ginger and pickle and stir over medium heat for 1 minute. Add the carrots, scallion whites, salt, and water. Bring to a boil and simmer gently for 35 minutes. Add the cucumber, stock, and crumbled stock cube. Continue to cook and simmer for a further 5–6 minutes. Adjust the seasonings, sprinkle with the scallion greens, and serve.

## SQUASH (OR WINTER MELON) SOUP WITH DRIED MUSHROOMS

This is another Chinese soup whose character is determined by the amount of a specific vegetable used. It is also another satisfying soup to consume with quantities of rice.

Serves 4–5

2 pounds squash
6–7 medium-sized Chinese
  dried mushrooms
2½ tablespoons vegetable oil
4 slices ginger root
1½ teaspoons salt
3 cups water

2 cups double-strained vegetarian stock
1 vegetarian stock cube
1½ tablespoons light soy
  sauce
salt and pepper

Clean and peel the squash and cut into 2½-by-1-by-½-inch pieces. Soak the dried mushrooms in hot water for half an hour and drain, reserving the water. Remove and discard the stems and cut the caps into shreds.

Heat the oil in a saucepan or wok. When hot, add the ginger, salt, and mushrooms. Stir-fry for 1 minute. Add the water, mushroom water, and squash. Bring to a boil and simmer gently for 40 minutes. Add the stock, crumbled stock cube, and soy sauce. Simmer gently for a further 10 minutes. Add salt and pepper to taste and serve.

# VEGETABLE STEM SOUP
## WITH BRAISED BAMBOO SHOOTS
## AND SALTED TURNIPS

The vegetable stems should be very tender, almost melting in the mouth, yet be redolent with vegetable flavor. Another excellent soup to consume with quantities of rice.

*Serves 4–5*

8 ounces broccoli stems
8 ounces Chinese cabbage
  stems
half a cauliflower stem
2 ounces braised bamboo
  shoots (available in cans)
2 ounces salted turnips (available in cans or jars)
2½ tablespoons vegetable oil

3 slices ginger root
½ teaspoon salt
3 cups water
2 cups double-strained vegetarian stock
1½ tablespoons light soy
  sauce
1½ vegetarian stock cubes
salt and pepper

Since the tops and leaves of the vegetables can be used for other purposes, the stems can be cut out and carved into thick double-mahjong-size pieces. Cut the bamboo shoots into thin 1-inch strips. Rinse the salted turnips in running water and cut into 1-inch strips.

Heat the oil in a saucepan or wok. When hot, add the ginger, bamboo shoots, and salted turnips. Stir-fry for 1 minute. Add the salt, water, and all the vegetable stems. Bring to a boil and simmer gently for 30 minutes. Add the vegetarian stock, soy sauce, and crumbled stock cubes. Stir and cook gently for a further 5–6 minutes. Add salt and pepper to taste and serve.

# THREE SHREDDED INGREDIENTS AND TRANSPARENT NOODLE SOUP

This is considered a more refined soup than the previous recipes, in which the vegetables are cut and cooked in chunky pieces, and is often served at dinner parties. The contrast of flavor and texture of the different ingredients all awash in a savory soup gives the palate a uniquely satisfying sensation.

Serves 4–5

3–4 ounces Chinese braised bamboo shoots
3–4 ounces celery
5–6 medium-sized Chinese dried mushrooms
2 ounces transparent bean-starch noodles
2 tablespoons vegetable oil
3 slices ginger root

2 cups water
1 teaspoon salt
1 vegetarian stock cube
1½ cups double-strained vegetarian stock
1 tablespoon light soy sauce
salt and pepper
1 teaspoon sesame oil

Cut the bamboo shoots and celery into matchstick strips. Soak the dried mushrooms in hot water for half an hour and drain, reserving the mushroom water. Remove and discard the stems and cut the caps into similar strips. Soak the noodles in warm water for 5–6 minutes and cut into sections 3 inches long.

Heat the oil in a saucepan or wok. When hot add the ginger and dried mushrooms and stir-fry for 1 minute. Add the water, salt, crumbled stock cube, noodles, shredded bamboo shoots, and celery. Bring to a boil and simmer gently for 12 minutes. Add the stock, mushroom water, and soy sauce and continue to simmer for a further 3–4 minutes. Add salt and pepper to taste, sprinkle with the sesame oil, and serve.

# THREE MUSHROOM SOUP WITH TRANSPARENT BEAN-STARCH NOODLES

This is a refined soup. It should be very savory and full of mushroom flavor, with the bamboo shoots and noodles providing added interest and contrast in texture.

Serves 4–5

8 ounces firm button mushrooms
5–6 medium-sized Chinese
dried mushrooms
1½–2 ounces European dried
mushrooms (available in
packets)
2 ounces winter bamboo
shoots
2 ounces transparent bean-
starch noodles

2 tablespoons vegetable oil
1 teaspoon salt
2 slices ginger root
4–5 ounces Chinese straw
mushrooms
1½ cups water
2 cups double-strained vegetarian stock
1 vegetarian stock cube
1 tablespoon light soy sauce
1 teaspoon sesame oil

Cut the button mushrooms into ¼-inch slices. Soak the Chinese dried mushrooms in ½ cup hot water for half an hour and drain, reserving the water. Remove and discard the stems and cut the caps into quarters. Similarly soak the European dried mushrooms in ½ cup hot water for half an hour and drain, reserving the water. Coarsely chop or slice them, stems and all. Cut the bamboo shoots into matchstick strips. Soak the noodles in water, drain, and cut into 2-inch sections.

Heat the oil in a saucepan or wok. When hot, add all the dried mushrooms, the salt, and the ginger. Stir-fry for 1½ minutes. Add the button mushrooms, straw mushrooms, bamboo shoots, and the 1½ cups water. Bring to a boil and simmer gently for 10 minutes.

Add the noodles, stock, crumbled stock cube, soy sauce, and mushroom water. Stir and mix the ingredients together, bring to a boil, and simmer for another 3–4 minutes. Sprinkle with sesame oil and serve.

## ASPARAGUS SOUP WITH NEEDLE MUSHROOMS AND FRIED BEAN CURD STRIPS

Apart from its flavor, this soup is interesting in that its main ingredients all have such different shapes and textures to intrigue the palate.

Serves 4–5

1–1½ pounds fresh asparagus
1 cake bean curd
vegetable oil for deep-frying
1½ tablespoons snow pickle
1 small onion
2½ tablespoons vegetable oil
2 cups water
1 vegetarian stock cube

4–6 ounces needle mushrooms (available canned from Chinese foodstores)
1 teaspoon sugar
1½ cups double-strained vegetarian stock
1 teaspoon salt
1 tablespoon light soy sauce
2 tablespoons dry sherry

Rinse and trim the asparagus and cut it slantwise into 2-inch sections. Cut the bean curd into double sugar-lump-sized rectangular pieces. Deep-fry them for 2½ minutes or until slightly brown. Drain well. Coarsely chop the pickle and onion.

Heat the oil in a saucepan or wok. Add the chopped pickle and onion and stir-fry over medium heat for 1 minute. Add the asparagus and stir-fry with the other ingredients for 2 minutes. Add the water, crumbled stock cube, mushrooms, and sugar. Bring to a boil and simmer gently for 20 minutes. Pour in the stock and add the bean curd, salt, soy sauce, and sherry. Continue to simmer for 5 minutes and serve.

## HOT AND SOUR SOUP

This soup has considerable body. It is very popular in north and central China during the colder months; a bowlful will have a very warming effect in winter anywhere.

Serves 4–5

2½ tablespoons Sichuan Ja Tsai pickle
3 slices ginger root
1 medium-sized onion
1½ ounces wood ears
5 medium-sized Chinese dried mushrooms
3 ounces braised bamboo shoots
1 ounce bean curd skin (optional)
2 scallions
1½ cakes bean curd
2 eggs
2½ tablespoons vegetable oil
1¾ cups water

1 teaspoon salt
5 tablespoons straw mushrooms
2 cups vegetarian stock
2 vegetarian stock cubes
3–4 tablespoons green peas
SAUCE:
2 tablespoons cornstarch blended in 5 tablespoons water
4 tablespoons wine vinegar
3 tablespoons water
1 tablespoon dry sherry
2 tablespoons light soy sauce
¼ teaspoon freshly ground black pepper

Cut the pickle and ginger into fine shreds, and the onion into thin slices. Rinse the wood ears well. Soak the dried mushrooms in hot water for half an hour, drain, remove and discard the stems, and cut the caps into shreds. Cut the bamboo shoots and bean curd skin into matchstick strips. Cut the scallions into ¼-inch shavings, separating the whites from the greens. Cut the bean curd into sugar-lump-sized cubes. Beat the eggs lightly in a bowl.

Mix the ingredients for the sauce together until well blended. Heat the oil in a saucepan or wok. When hot, add the pickle, ginger, and dried mushrooms. Stir over medium heat for 1½ minutes. Add the water and salt. When contents come to a boil, add the wood ears, straw mushrooms, bamboo shoots, scallion whites, bean curd skin, and stock. Bring back to a boil, reduce heat, and simmer gently for 10 minutes. Stir in the crumbled stock cubes and add the bean curd, peas, and scallion greens. Cook gently for a further 3 minutes. Slowly pour in the sauce mixture, stirring all the while, which will cause the soup to thicken. Drip the beaten egg in a fine stream over the surface of the soup. When it sets, the soup is ready to serve.

# 6 NOODLES

The three main types of Chinese noodles are made of wheat flour, rice flour, and bean flour, and they are generally cooked in three different ways: fried noodles, or chow mein, are stir-fried with other ingredients in a pan or wok; cooked noodles, or noodles in gravy, are cooked in a pot with sauce or gravy; while soup noodles are cooked and suspended in soup. All noodle dishes are considered to be snacks and are consumed on their own as a small meal at odd times during the day. They can also be added to the dishes served during a meal to augment it; or they can be served as a soup to start or, more usually, to finish a meal. Wheat-flour noodles are the common noodles of the north, where the climate is too dry for growing rice; in the south and along the Yangtze valley, where rice is abundantly grown, half the noodles consumed are made of rice flour. Bean-flour noodles are a special category; they are very white in color but become almost transparent when cooked. Unlike other noodles prepared and eaten as bulk food, they are cooked as a savory dish, served with several other savory dishes on the table, and eaten with rice. They are very rarely served as a snack entirely on their own.

# TRANSPARENT BEAN-STARCH NOODLES

## ANTS CLIMBING THE TREE
### (MA-YI SAN SHU)

This is one of the best-known bean-flour noodle dishes—very savory and aromatic and excellent with rice.

*Serves 4–5, with other dishes*

5–6 ounces transparent bean-starch noodles

5 medium-sized Chinese dried mushrooms

2 cloves garlic

2 tablespoons Sichuan Ja Tsai pickle

3 ounces braised bamboo shoots (available canned)

4–5 tablespoons roasted peanuts

2 scallions

4½ tablespoons vegetable oil

1 teaspoon salt

3–4 tablespoons green peas

1½ teaspoons sesame oil

SAUCE:

4 tablespoons vegetarian stock

¼ teaspoon salt

1 tablespoon light soy sauce

½ vegetarian stock cube

1 tablespoon wine vinegar

1½ tablespoons dry sherry

Soak the bean-starch noodles in hot water for 6–7 minutes, drain, and cut with scissors into sections 3–4 inches long. Soak the dried mushrooms in hot water for half an hour, drain, remove and discard the stems, and coarsely chop the caps. Crush and chop the garlic, and coarsely chop the pickle and bamboo shoots. Crush and pound the roasted peanuts. Cut the scallions into fine shavings, separating the whites from the greens. Mix the sauce ingredients together until well blended.

Heat 4 tablespoons of the vegetable oil in a large frying pan or wok. When hot, add the chopped pickle, garlic, salt, bamboo shoots, dried mushrooms, and scallion whites and stir-fry over medium heat for 2 minutes. Add the noodles and turn and mix them well with the other ingredients for 2 minutes. Pour the sauce evenly over the contents and continue to stir, mix, and turn over medium heat for a further 2 minutes. Remove the contents and transfer to a serving dish.

Add the remaining vegetable oil to the pan or wok. When hot, add the crushed peanuts and stir for half a minute, followed by the peas and scallion greens. Stir them all together for half a minute. Sprinkle these and the sesame oil evenly over the noodles in the dish.

## COOKED TRANSPARENT BEAN-STARCH NOODLES WITH FRESH VEGETABLES

This dish is full of vegetable qualities that are enhanced by the contrasting character of the very savory noodles. It can be eaten on its own, but the Chinese are more likely to have it as an accompaniment to rice.

Serves 4–5, with other dishes

5–6 ounces transparent bean-
  starch noodles
2 cloves garlic
3 slices ginger root
2 scallions

3–4 ounces green beans
3–4 ounces broccoli tops
3–4 ounces asparagus spears
3–4 ounces bean sprouts
3 tablespoons vegetable oil

1 teaspoon salt
1 cup double-strained vege-
    tarian stock
1 vegetarian stock cube

4 tablespoons white wine
1½ tablespoons light soy
    sauce
1 teaspoon sesame oil

Soak the noodles in hot water for 7–8 minutes, drain, and cut with scissors into sections 3–4 inches long. Coarsely crush and chop the garlic. Shred the ginger, and cut the scallions into ¼-inch shavings, separating the white parts from the green. Rinse and trim the beans, the broccoli, and the asparagus into 1½–2-inch sections.

Heat the oil in a large saucepan or wok. When hot, add the garlic, ginger, scallion whites, and salt. Stir-fry over medium heat for 1½ minutes. Add all the other vegetables. Stir and turn them with the other ingredients for 3 minutes. Add the stock, and sprinkle with the crumbled stock cube. Bring to a boil and simmer gently for 3 minutes. Add the noodles, which will soak up all the liquid in the pan or wok. Reduce the heat and simmer slowly for a further 4–5 minutes, stirring and turning now and then. Sprinkle with the wine, soy sauce, and sesame oil. Stir, turn once more, and serve.

## TRANSPARENT BEAN-STARCH NOODLES WITH EGG SAUCE

This is one of the very few occasions when bean-starch noodles are served on their own, rather than being eaten with rice.

Serves 4–5, with 1 or 2 other dishes

4–5 ounces bean-starch
    noodles
2 slices ginger root
3 scallions

4 eggs
2½ tablespoons vegetable oil
½ teaspoon salt
2 cups vegetarian stock

1½ tablespoons butter or
  margarine
SAUCE:
2 tablespoons light soy sauce

3 tablespoons dry sherry
1 tablespoon red bean curd
  "cheese"
2 tablespoons vegetarian stock

Soak the noodles in hot water for 7–8 minutes, drain, and cut with scissors into sections 3–4 inches long. Cut the ginger into fine shreds, and the scallions into ½-inch sections. Beat the eggs lightly with a fork or chopsticks for 10–12 seconds. Mix the sauce ingredients together until well blended.

Heat the oil in a saucepan or wok. When hot, add the ginger, salt, and scallion whites. Stir for half a minute. Add half the beaten eggs. Stir until the eggs set. Pour in the stock and the sauce mixture. Stir until the contents boil. Add butter or margarine and the remainder of the beaten eggs. Stir quickly and remove from the heat before the eggs are completely set. Sprinkle with the scallion greens.

Divide the noodles into 4–5 bowls and pour some of the sauce over the contents of each bowl of noodles.

# BUDDHIST DELIGHT (LO-HAN JAI)

This is one of the most popular vegetarian dishes, which is served in Chinese temples and monasteries. There are always hundreds of enshrined minor gods, called "Lo-Hans," who presumably have to be fed. The dish is prepared by stewing together a variety of dried vegetables with a range of fresh vegetables, together with bean-starch noodles cooked in a sauce made from stock and seasoned with a few flavoring agents.

As this is a very large dish with lots of ingredients, it will have to be served in a very large serving bowl. This is placed at the center of the table for diners to help themselves from with both chopsticks and a serving spoon.

Serves 8–10

DRIED INGREDIENTS:
6 medium-sized Chinese dried
mushrooms
3 tablespoons wood ears
3 tablespoons hair seaweed
2 ounces dried bamboo shoots
3 ounces dried chestnuts
3 lily bud stems
2 dried bean curd sticks
4 slices lotus roots or gingko
nuts
3–4 tablespoons lotus nuts
4–5 ounces bean-starch
noodles
1 teaspoon salt
3 tablespoons vegetable oil
FRESH INGREDIENTS:
1 stick celery, shredded
1 medium-sized sweet pepper,
shredded
2 ounces fresh mushrooms,
shredded

2 scallions, cut into 1-inch
sections
2–3 ounces bean sprouts,
blanched
2–3 ounces Chinese white
cabbage, shredded
2–3 ounces cauliflower, broken into small florets
2–3 ounces broccoli, broken
into small florets
2½ tablespoons vegetable oil
½ teaspoon salt
2 teaspoons sesame oil
STOCK AND SAUCE:
2 cups vegetarian stock
2½ tablespoons light soy
sauce
¼ teaspoon salt
1 tablespoon bean curd
"cheese"
1½ tablespoons rice wine or
sherry

Soak the mushrooms in hot water for half an hour, drain, remove and discard the stems, and cut the caps into quarters. Rinse, soak in warm water, and drain wood ears. Rinse the hair seaweed, soak for 5 minutes in warm water, and drain. Rinse the bamboo shoots, soak in warm water for 15 minutes, drain, and cut into 2-inch sections. Soak the dried chestnuts in warm water for half an hour and cut into halves. Soak the lily bud stems in warm water for 5 minutes and cut into 2-inch sections. Break the bean curd sticks into 2-inch sections, soak in hot water for 25 minutes, and drain. Soak the bean-starch noodles in warm water for 7–8 minutes and cut into 3-inch sections.

Cook the dried ingredients (except for the bean-starch noodles) and fresh ingredients by stir-frying them in oil in two separate saucepans or woks. Stir-fry for 3–3½ minutes each. Put the ingredients together in one saucepan or wok. Pour in the stock and stir in the soy sauce, salt, bean curd "cheese," and rice wine or sherry. Bring contents to a boil and simmer gently for 6–7 minutes. Add the bean-starch noodles, turn and stir, and mix evenly with the other ingredients in the pan or wok. Bring back to a boil, reduce the heat, and simmer gently for another 6–7 minutes. Sprinkle with sesame oil and serve.

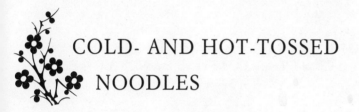

# COLD- AND HOT-TOSSED NOODLES

Cold-tossed noodles are a hot-weather dish, eaten often throughout China in the summer. They can be served with a single sauce poured over the noodles and stirred into them, or with several sauces placed on the table so that diners can help themselves to whatever sauce or sauces they would like to mix into their own bowl of noodles. Since we Chinese treat noodles as a form of bulk food like rice, to which savory foods or sauces have to be added to make them more appealing, most of the relishes and sauces that go well with rice can also be applied to noodles (see pages 120–28). Usually, in addition to small platefuls of pickles, salted and marinated vegetables, and sauces such as mushroom, Sichuan eggplant and bamboo shoot, tomato and black bean, or egg and butter bean, which should be provided in bowls on the table, there should be a bowlful of mixed peanut butter with sesame oil, stock and soya sauce (6 tablespoons peanut butter, 4 tablespoons salad oil, 2 tablespoons sesame oil, 3 tablespoons light soy sauce, 1 tablespoon red chili oil, and 3 tablespoons double-strained vegetarian stock), one large bowlful each of shredded cucumber and well-washed and drained bean sprouts, and one smaller bowl or dish of finely shredded ginger in aromatic vinegar. The diners should be provided with their own individual bowls of parboiled noodles. They help themselves to pinches of the relishes and spoonfuls of one or more of the sauces, which should be poured on top of the noodles, with a thin spread of bean sprouts and shredded cucumber. To add more zest to the dish, a spoonful of aromatic vinegar with shredded ginger may be scattered over it all before tossing and mixing all the ingredients together with the noodles and eating them in mouthfuls with gusto. Cold-tossed noodles served in this way can be a fascinating and inexpensive way of starting a dinner party.

## COLD-TOSSED NOODLES WITH SWEETENED BROWN BEAN SAUCE (SOY JAM SAUCE)

Strictly speaking, this dish should be called "warm-tossed noodles," as, except for the shredded vegetables, the ingredients could be luke-warm.

To parboil the noodles, cook them in boiling water (4–5 minutes for fresh or 7–8 minutes for dried, depending upon the noodles; 14–15 minutes if using spaghetti) until barely done. The noodles should then be quickly rinsed under running water and drained. A small amount of vegetable oil (about 1½ teaspoons) should then be sprinkled and stirred into them to keep them from sticking. They can either be used as they are or they can be heated up by immersing them in boiling water for 15–20 seconds. For 4–5 portions, 1¼ pounds dried or 1¾ pounds fresh noodles will be required.

For 4–5 servings, a bowlful of Soy Jam Sauce, or Sweetened Brown Bean Sauce, can be prepared by heating 5–6 tablespoons Brown Bean Sauce with 3–4 tablespoons sugar, 1½ tablespoons vegetable oil, 1½ tablespoons finely chopped ginger, 2 tablespoons soy sauce, and 1 cup water. Heat all the ingredients together in a saucepan or wok, stirring all the time over medium heat, until the liquid has been reduced by between a third and a half. The sauce obtained should be poured into a large or medium bowl and set on the table together with 3 or 4 other bowls containing bean sprouts, shredded cucumber, shredded egg pancake, chopped scallions, and chopped coriander. The first three items should be contained in large bowls and the last two in small to medium bowls. These bowls of ingredients should also be supported by an additional small to medium bowl of aromatic vinegar or wine vinegar.

The diner sprinkles his or her bowl of noodles with 2 tablespoons of sauce and spreads over them a thin coating of shredded vegetables. Another tablespoon of sauce and one of vinegar are sprinkled on top of the vegetables before tossing them all together. Because of the rich sharpness of the sauce and the crunchiness of the vegetables cushioned against the firm softness of the noodles, any diner will dig into such a bowl of noodles with considerable satisfaction.

## HOT-TOSSED NOODLES WITH SESAME (OR PEANUT BUTTER) SAUCE

The diner sprinkes his or her own bowl of hot noodles with chopped scallions, then places 2–3 tablespoons of peanut butter sauce on top. When the freshly chopped scallions and sauce are stirred into the hot noodles, they generate a unique fragrance, highly appealing to both the nostrils and the palate. As with eating roasted peanuts, most people, given the opportunity, tend to eat more than they bargained for.

Serves 3–4

1 pound dried noodles (or 1½ pounds fresh)

4 scallions
5–6 tablespoons peanut butter

2 tablespoons sesame oil

3 tablespoons vegetable oil

3 tablespoons light soy sauce

4 tablespoons warm

vegetarian stock

Parboil the noodles in the same manner as in the previous recipe. Heat them just before serving by immersing in boiling water for 10–12 seconds. Drain thoroughly. Divide the noodles among the diners' individual bowls.

Finely chop the scallions. Mix the peanut butter, sesame and vegetable oils, soy sauce, and stock together until well blended. Serve the chopped scallions and sauce in separate bowls.

## CASSEROLE OF COOKED NOODLES WITH FOUR SOY-BRAISED CHUNKY VEGETABLES, AND SEMI-SOUP DISH OF MUSHROOMS, PICKLES, CUCUMBER, AND CABBAGE

Serves 4–5

To prepare this composite dish, put both the ready-cooked dishes (see pages 87, 94) in a casserole, add 1 cup of vegetarian stock, 1½ tablespoons soy sauce, and 2 tablespoons red or white wine and bring the contents to a boil. Simmer for 5–6 minutes, then stir in 1½ tablespoons of cornstarch blended with 4 tablespoons of water to thicken the sauce. Once the sauce has thickened, add 1¼–1½ pounds parboiled noodles to the casserole and cook gently with the other ingredients for about 3–4 minutes. Once the noodles are heated through, the dish is ready to serve.

The aim is not to impregnate the noodles with the flavor of the sauce and other ingredients, but for them to act as a bland buffer that sets off the savoriness against the firm, satisfying texture of the noodles themselves.

# FRIED NOODLES, OR CHOW MEIN

Fried noodles are really parboiled noodles that have been stir-fried with a savory stir-fried dish (in our case, a savory stir-fried vegetable dish). *Chow* means "stir-fry" and *mein* is "noodles." To make a dish of chow mein, parboiled noodles are stir-fried and mixed with half the ingredients of a stir-fried dish in order to give the noodles an overall savoriness. The noodles are topped with a hot garnish made from the remaining half of the stir-fried dish. This should be given an extra stir and turn over high heat for a minute or two in a frying pan or wok. The dish will expand in bulk quite considerably because of the noodles, so you will need to add one tablespoon each of oil and soy sauce at both stages of stir-frying. An average stir-fried dish (see pages 69–82) should be sufficient with 1 pound dried or 1½ pounds fresh noodles for 3–4 portions of fried noodles, or chow mein.

Chow mein is very frequently served in restaurants, since in restaurant kitchens there are often leftover bits and pieces of raw foods which can be added to ready-cooked dishes to make excellent chow mein. When food materials are cut small and subjected to high-heat stir-frying, they release and generate flavor that can in turn be transmitted to bulk foods such as noodles, making them much more appealing and palatable.

## FRIED NOODLES, OR CHOW MEIN, WITH STIR-FRIED SNOW PEAS, BABY CORN, DRIED MUSHROOMS, AND WOOD EARS

This recipe is an example of using a ready-cooked dish to prepare fried noodles, or chow mein, which can be served on its own as a complete meal.

Serves 3–4

1 pound dried or 1⅓ pounds
   fresh noodles
4 medium-sized dried
   mushrooms
1 medium-sized onion
3 tablespoons vegetable oil

4 ounces stir-fried snow peas
4 ounces canned baby corn
2 tablespoons wood ears
3 tablespoons soy sauce
2 tablespoons dry sherry

Prepare the noodles by parboiling them (dried noodles for 7–8 minutes, or fresh noodles for 4–5 minutes). Drain, rinse under running water, and drain again thoroughly. Soak the dried mushrooms in hot water for half an hour and drain, reserving the mushroom water. Cut the onion into very thin slices.

Heat 2 tablespoons of the oil in a large frying pan or wok. Add the onion and half the stir-fried snow peas, baby corn, mushrooms, and wood ears and stir over medium heat for 2 minutes. Add the noodles, spreading them out over the ingredients in the pan or wok. Sprinkle with 1½ tablespoons of the soy sauce and the mushroom water and stir-fry for 2½ minutes. Transfer to a well-heated serving dish.

Add the remaining tablespoon of oil to the same pan or wok. Add the balance of the stir-fried snow peas, baby corn, mushrooms, and wood ears to the pan. Sprinkle with the sherry and the balance of the soy sauce. Stir-fry over high heat for 1 minute. Transfer the contents and use them as garnish on top of the noodles in the serving dish. If there are any bits and pieces of fresh food that need using up, they can be sliced or chopped small and added to the pan with the onion slices at the beginning of the stir-frying to provide additional flavor.

## CRISPY NOODLE NESTS

Fried noodles, or chow mein, are sometimes served in "nests." These can be made quite easily, and they make a very picturesque presentation.

The nests are made by parboiling the noodles in the usual manner—dry noodles for 7–8 minutes, fresh noodles for 3–4 minutes (noodles for this purpose can be underboiled by ½–1 minute). After the noodles have been softened by boiling, drain and spread them out evenly in one layer to cover the bottom of a metal sieve. Sprinkle the top of the still moist noodles lightly with 1 tablespoon of cornstarch. Spread another layer of noodles on top of the first layer and press the top layer down with the aid of another metal sieve of about the same size as, or slightly smaller than, the first.

All that needs to be done now is to submerge the sieves with the flattened noodles in hot boiling oil for 2–3 minutes. When the noodles are golden brown and crispy, drain and remove the sieves. The noodles will be shaped like cups or nests that can be used to contain and serve any stir-fried dish, providing its sauce is not too runny. To steady the nests (since they all contain some sauce), it is best to place them inside a bowl before pouring the stir-fried dish into them.

# BRAISED MUSHROOM NOODLES WITH SNOW PEAS AND QUAIL EGGS, SERVED IN A NOODLE NEST

This large crispy noodle nest, filled to the brim with noodles and mushrooms and decorated with the green of the snow peas and the quail eggs, is an extremely picturesque sight and almost looks like a real bird's nest, full of food for the young and topped by a few bird's eggs.

Serves 3–4

5–6 medium-sized Chinese dried mushrooms
3–4 ounces snow peas
2 slices ginger root
4 quail eggs
3 tablespoons vegetable oil
¼ teaspoon salt
1 teaspoon sugar
1 large noodle nest (see page 157)
4–5 ounces Chinese straw mushrooms
4–5 ounces white button mushrooms

4–5 tablespoons double-strained vegetarian stock
1½ tablespoons light soy sauce
1 tablespoon butter
4 tablespoons white wine
1 pinch pepper
¾ tablespoon cornstarch blended in 3 tablespoons water
1 pound parboiled noodles (tossed with 1½ teaspoons vegetable oil to prevent sticking)

Soak the Chinese dried mushrooms in hot water for half an hour and drain, reserving the mushroom water. Remove and discard the stems and cut the caps into quarters. Rinse and trim the snow peas and cut them diagonally across the middle into halves. Cut the ginger into shreds. Boil the quail eggs for 3½ minutes and shell. Clean and trim the button mushrooms and cut them through the caps and stems into halves or quarters.

Heat the oil in a frying pan or wok. When hot, add the ginger and dried mushrooms. Stir for 1½ minutes. Add the snow peas, salt, and sugar. Pour in the reserved mushroom water. Stir-fry all the ingredients together for 1 minute. Cook over medium heat for a further 2 minutes. Remove the mushrooms and snow peas with a perforated spoon and place half of them in the noodle nest, lining the bottom and sides.

Add the straw mushrooms and button mushrooms to the remaining sauce in the pan or wok. When contents start to boil, add the stock, soy sauce, butter, wine, and pepper. Bring back to a boil, reduce heat, and simmer gently for 3–4 minutes. Stir in the blended corn-starch, which will thicken the sauce. Add the parboiled noodles to the sauce and turn and stir with the rest of the ingredients in the pan or wok. When the noodles have heated through and are evenly coated with the sauce, transfer them (with a metal spoon and the help of a pair of chopsticks) to fill the noodle nest. Gradually build up the noodles and mushrooms in the nest, layer by layer, pouring the residual sauce over them, using the remaining snow peas and dried mushrooms and the quail eggs to decorate the sides and top of the noodles.

## CRISPY RICE-FLOUR NOODLES

Crispy noodles look like vermicelli, are gray-white in color, and can be bought in ½-pound packets. They are not served on their own but are usually eaten with soft-fried noodles to provide a contrast of texture in the same dish. The crispy noodles form a bed on a large serving dish, and a dish of freshly cooked soft-fried noodles is spread on top. Not infrequently a portion of crispy noodles is broken up into smaller pieces and sprinkled on top of the soft-fried noodles to produce a crouton effect. Thus the soft-fried savory noodles are served in between two layers of crispy noodles. The diner stirs and mixes together the two types of noodles, with their contrasting textures, and it is this interplay of textures that intrigues the palate.

These light crispy noodles can be made very quickly as follows:

Serves 4–6

8 ounces rice-flour noodles                vegetable oil for shallow-
frying or deep-frying (2–4 cups)

Divide the rice-flour noodles into 4–6 portions, so that you fry only one portion at a time (immediately after hitting the hot oil, the noodles will rise and almost explode into a white mass of crispy noodles ten or more times their original volume).

Heat the oil in a frying pan or wok over medium heat for 1½ minutes, or until a crumb will sizzle audibly when dropped into it.

Drop the rice-flour noodles into the hot oil. Remove with a large perforated spoon and place them on absorbent paper to remove any excess grease. Repeat the procedure until you have obtained the right quantity of crispy noodles. Some chefs would crush these crispy noodles before laying them out as a bed for a dish of soft-fried noodles, or chow mein (page 156), but I prefer to spread them out lightly in a single layer on a large serving dish. You can mix together the crispy and soft noodles as you eat, rather than stirring them all up together from the start.

## DOUBLE-BROWNED NOODLES (LIANG MEIN HUANG)

Serves 4–5

These are shallow-fried (usually egg) noodles which come in pads of about 2½–3 inches in diameter. They are first boiled for 3–4 minutes, and when softened they are loosened out into a thick pancake. This noodle pancake is then fried in a frying pan in a small amount of oil (about 2–3 tablespoons) until it begins to brown on one side, then turned or flipped over and fried with a bit more oil (1–1½ tablespoons) to brown on the other side. It is then transferred to a serving dish.

Although the noodles should be brown and crispy on both sides, they should still be fairly soft in between. The diner should be able to feel both the softness and the crispness of the noodles in each mouthful as he or she consumes the dish. Almost any savory stir-fried dish with thick sauce can be used to pour over these double-browned noodles as toppings to complete the dish.

# A TOPPING FOR DOUBLE-BROWNED NOODLES

Serves 4–5

4–5 Chinese dried mushrooms
2 slices ginger root
3 ounces marinated bamboo shoots (available canned)
2 cloves garlic
2 scallions
3½ tablespoons vegetable oil
½ teaspoon salt
3–4 ounces bean sprouts
3 tablespoons green peas

4–5 tablespoons vegetarian stock
2 tablespoons soy sauce
½ vegetarian stock cube
2½ teaspoons cornstarch blended in 4 tablespoons water
1 teaspoon sesame oil
12 ounces double-browned noodles

Soak the mushrooms in ½ cup hot water for half an hour and drain, reserving half the mushroom water. Shred the ginger and bamboo shoots. Coarsely crush the garlic. Cut the scallions into ½-inch pieces, separating the whites from the greens.

Heat the oil in a frying pan or wok. When hot, add the mushrooms, ginger, garlic, and salt. Stir-fry for 1½ minutes over medium heat. Add the scallion whites, bean sprouts, peas, and bamboo shoots and continue to stir-fry for 1 more minute. Add the stock, mushroom water, soy sauce, and crumbled stock cube. Stir and cook them together for 3 minutes. Add the scallion greens and stir in the blended cornstarch. When the sauce thickens and becomes translucent, sprinkle with sesame oil.

Pour the contents from the pan or wok over the double-browned noodles in a serving dish. Since the noodle pancake, which has been browned on both sides, is quite firm, it is helpful for Westerners who may not be able to manage with chopsticks to cut the noodles into 5–6 pieces with a knife.

 # NOODLE SOUP

Noodle soup is as popular and as regularly served in China as chow mein or soft-fried noodles. In the winter, it might be even more widely served than fried noodles, as it is a much more warming and substantial dish. Noodle soup is not quite like other Chinese soups, which are meant to go with several other dishes as part of a composite meal; rather it is meant to stand on its own as a meal in itself.

A soup can be made into a noodle soup simply by adding noodles to soup during the last stages of cooking. But, generally speaking, for a soup to qualify as noodle soup a considerable amount of noodles has to be added (roughly 3–4 ounces cooked noodles per bowl). This greatly lowers the savoriness of the soup, since the added noodles are unseasoned. In order to maintain the savoriness of the dish, the soup will have to be pepped up with some flavoring ingredients. The most widely used are pickles, such as snow pickles, winter pickles, or hot Sichuan Ja Tsai pickles, in addition to dried mushrooms, dried shrimp, dried salted turnips, snow pickle, or dried kelp. It is only after the addition of these ingredients that flavoring agents such as soy sauce, hoisin sauce, chili sauce, or vegetarian stock cubes can also be added to further vary the seasoning. Once the general level of the seasoning and savoriness of the soup has been raised, the cooked noodles may then be added to heat up in the soup for a few minutes with the other ingredients before the dish can be served. Again, the reason for cooking the noodles in the soup is not so much for the noodles to absorb the flavor of the soup as to provide a bland contrast, which will increase the appreciation of the soup itself.

However, there are soups, like Hot and Sour Soup (page 31), that because of their high seasoning and savoriness in the first place produce a substantial and acceptable noodle soup using 4 ounces plain boiled noodles to 1 cup soup; but most other soups require the addition of a certain amount of dried, salted, or pickled flavoring ingredients and sauces before the plain boiled noodles are added. The following recipes are examples.

## SPINACH AND BRAISED BAMBOO SHOOT NOODLE SOUP

The noodle soup should be divided evenly into 4–5 large bowls to be served to individual diners. The enjoyment of consuming such a large bowl of noodle soup is the combination of digging into the noodles and drinking the savory soup.

Serves 4 as a large snack or a complete meal

1½ pounds noodles (dried or fresh)
2 tablespoons vegetable oil
2–3 tablespoons snow pickle, coarsely chopped

2 scallions
4 portions Spinach and Braised Bamboo Shoot Soup (pages 131–32)
2 tablespoons light soy sauce

163

Boil the dried noodles for 5–6 minutes, or the fresh for 3–4 minutes, and drain. Heat the oil in a saucepan or wok. When hot, add the pickle and scallions. Stir-fry for 1½ minutes. Add the soup and soy sauce. Bring to a boil, reduce the heat, and simmer for 2 minutes. Add the noodles, stirring them evenly into the soup. Cook gently for a further 2–3 minutes and the noodle soup is ready to serve.

## CHINESE WHITE CABBAGE NOODLE SOUP WITH TOMATO AND BLACK BEAN SAUCE

This dish should not only be satisfying to consume but should also be very appealing visually.

*Serves 4–5 as a large snack or a complete meal*

2 tablespoons vegetable oil
2 tablespoons snow pickle, coarsely chopped
2–3 cloves garlic, crushed and coarsely chopped
1 cup vegetarian stock
½ vegetarian stock cube

4–5 portions Chinese White Cabbage Soup (pages 135–36)
1½ pounds cooked noodles
4–5 tablespoons Tomato and Black Bean Sauce (page 126)

Heat the oil in a saucepan or wok. When hot, add the pickle and garlic and stir-fry for almost a minute. Pour in the stock and sprinkle with the crumbled stock cube. Bring to a boil, stir a few times, then add the soup. Bring back to a boil and add the noodles. Allow 2–3 minutes for the noodles to heat through and the contents to simmer together. Transfer to a large serving bowl and top with heated Tomato and Black Bean Sauce. Allow the diners to help themselves from the common serving bowl.

# VEGETABLE STEM AND NOODLE SOUP WITH MUSHROOM SAUCE

Serves 4 as a large snack or a complete meal

2 tablespoons vegetable oil
1½ tablespoons Sichuan Ja
  Tsai pickle, coarsely
  chopped
2 tablespoons snow pickle,
  coarsely chopped
1 medium-sized onion,
  coarsely chopped
1 cup vegetarian stock

½ vegetarian stock cube
4 portions Vegetable Stem
  Soup (page 139)
1½ pounds cooked noodles
4–5 tablespoons Mushroom
  Sauce (page 124)
2 tablespoons coriander
  leaves, chopped (optional)

Heat the oil in a saucepan or wok. When hot, add the pickles and onion and stir over medium heat for 2 minutes. Pour in the stock and sprinkle with the crumbled stock cube. Bring to a boil, add the soup and the noodles, and simmer for 4–5 minutes.

Serve as in the previous recipe in a large communal serving bowl, topped with heated Mushroom Sauce, and sprinkled with 2 tablespoons of chopped coriander leaves if you like.

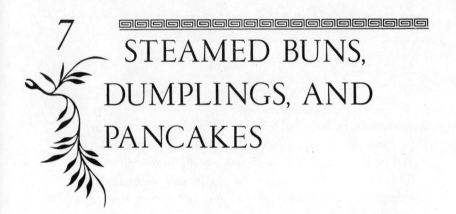

# 7

# STEAMED BUNS, DUMPLINGS, AND PANCAKES

Besides noodles, the other most important Chinese pastas are the steamed buns and dumplings. The simplest of Chinese steamed buns are the plain, unstuffed *man tou*. In north China, in school and college dining halls and workers' canteens, these *man tou* are provided steaming in baskets or in shallow metal buckets for the diners to help themselves from, and are consumed with rice and savory dishes which are served on the table.

In the south, however, no steamed buns are provided at mealtimes, and only rice is served. The buns are eaten only as snacks between meals, and then they are generally stuffed with fillings. Few southerners would appreciate solid steamed buns with no filling at all. Unstuffed steamed buns are really made to be eaten with stewed dishes, when there are gravies and sauces to be soaked up; or they are consumed with crispy dishes where the softness of the dough provides a welcome cushion to the crackling of deep-fried foods. But southerners are more used to and appreciative of the stuffed variety of buns and dumplings, which, like the Western sandwich or hamburger, are portable and convenient to eat on journeys or picnics.

On occasions such as a party or a banquet, where solid steamed buns might appear too heavy and unrefined, these dough products are made into steamed "flower rolls" and "silver thread" rolls, which, like the steamed *man tou* (or solid steamed buns), are served with stews or crispy and crackling dishes.

All this steamed pasta is made from raised dough, which is prepared in the following manner.

## YEAST DOUGH

For 1 pound plain flour use 1 teaspoon dry yeast dissolved in 2 tablespoons warm water. Allow 5–6 minutes for the yeast to dissolve completely. Add the flour and 1 tablespoon sugar to a large mixing bowl and mix them well together. Make a well in the center. Add the dissolved yeast, and pour in ⅔ cup lukewarm water. Stir with a wooden spoon until the flour and water are evenly mixed and form into a large lumpy ball. Turn the ball out onto a floured surface and knead it hard for 5–6 minutes. The dough and kneading surface may have to be floured a couple of times in the process. By the end of this time the dough should have become smooth and springy. Transfer the dough to a large covered bowl or pot to stand and rise for 2 hours in a warm part of the kitchen.

After 2 hours, place the risen dough again on a lightly floured surface and flatten it with the palm of your hand. Sprinkle the surface of the dough evenly with ½ teaspoon baking powder. Fold the dough over twice and knead it again, working it hard, for a further 5–6 minutes. It should now have become smooth and firm.

# PLAIN SOLID STEAMED BUNS, OR *MAN TOU*

Makes 8–10

Divide the yeast dough (see above) in two, and form each section into a large sausage-shaped strip about 6 inches long. Use your palms to help form regular-sized rolls. Use a knife to cut each roll into disks 1 inch thick. Arrange the disks on the floured surface of a tray and cover them all lightly with a cloth. Allow the dough pieces or disks to rise for about 45–50 minutes, when they should have become twice their original size.

Cover a large heatproof plate or tray with a damp cloth and evenly spread out these dough pieces on top. Insert the tray or plate into a steamer and steam vigorously for 15 minutes. Turn off the heat and allow the steamed buns to stand for a minute or two before removing and transferring them to a well-heated platter.

Although these steamed buns, or *man tou*, are no larger than the average Western rolls, because they are quite solid few people can eat more than three or four during a meal with savory dishes served. But they are very useful and satisfying to eat with plenty of sauce and gravy. These buns are often served with rice, and an average Chinese diner may eat a bun with a bowl or two of rice or a couple of buns with a bowl of rice. The weight-conscious Westerner would probably consume no more than half that amount.

# STEAMED "FLOWER ROLLS," OR
## *HUA JUAN*

For elegant people on more elaborate occasions the same dough used for plain steamed buns can be used to make the somewhat lighter "flower rolls."

Divide the dough in two. Roll each part into a rectangular sheet about 12 inches long by 8 inches wide. Brush the top of each sheet with 1 tablespoon sesame oil. Roll each dough sheet lengthwise firmly into the shape of a jelly roll about 1½ inches in diameter. Cut each roll crosswise into lengths of approximately 4 inches.

Place one roll on top of another, and press them together lightly. Use a chopstick to press down heavily across the center of the two rolls. This will cause the ends of the top roll to lift or open up (and on steaming, the edges of both top and bottom rolls will open up further, making them look like the petals of a flower). Continue until you have made a dozen of these "flower rolls." Line them up on a floured surface and cover them with a dry cloth. Let stand for about 45 minutes, by which time they should have doubled in size.

These "flower rolls" should be steamed vigorously in the same manner as the plain steamed buns, on top of a heatproof plate covered with a damp cloth, for about 15 minutes. Although these rolls weigh the same as the plain steamed buns, they look much lighter than the more solid buns. They are seldom eaten with rice (rice is not served during Chinese banquets, where there are often as many as a dozen courses of savory dishes) and therefore serve the purpose of counteracting the over-savoriness of a lengthy multi-course meal.

# STEAMED "SILVER THREAD" ROLLS

These are considered even more refined than the steamed "flower roll" buns in the previous recipe. They are also made by rolling out half the yeast dough into a thin rectangular sheet 12 by 8 inches. Cut the sheet into halves across the longer side. Divide one of the halves into two sheets for use as "wrappers." Brush the surface of the other half lightly with a small amount of sesame oil and fold it over. Use a sharp knife to cut this folded sheet of dough into matchstick-thin strips. Take up two strips at a time with your fingers and pull them gently until they are about 6 inches long. When you have finished cutting and pulling these dough strips into "dough threads," divide them into two lots. Roll and wrap them up tightly in the dough wrappers provided, tucking in the ends and allowing the weight of the roll to rest on the edge of the wrapper (the latter will cause the wrapper to seal during steaming). Allow these wrapped-up "silver thread" rolls to stand on greaseproof paper and rise for 45 minutes. When ready, arrange them on a heatproof plate, cover with a damp cloth, and steam vigorously for 20 minutes. Turn the heat off and allow them to stand in the steamer for 2 minutes before removing.

As these "silver thread" steamed rolls are over 6 inches long, they will need to be cut with a sharp knife into 3–4 slices across the dough threads on serving. Being made up of these innumerable "threads," these rolls absorb even more sauce or gravy than the average plain steamed buns, or "flower rolls." Hence they are often used at parties and banquets, in conjunction with stewed and long-braised foods, to add a measure of refinement to what might otherwise appear to be informal dishes.

## STUFFED STEAMED BUNS

These stuffed buns are probably one of the most popular and portable snacks of all Chinese food. They are "self-contained" (each bun contains both the bulk food and the savory filling), they can be conveniently carried, and they can be eaten hot or cold (like sandwiches). But, above all, they are pleasant to eat (the slight touch of sweetness in the dough contrasting with the savory saltiness of the filling seems to add to their appeal). Using the same yeast dough as on page 167, they are quite simple to make. The filling, however, will need to be cooked briefly first and then allowed to cool (preferably completely) before being stuffed into the dough, as the heating of the buns during steaming may not be sufficient to cook it.

*Makes 12 buns*

FOR THE STUFFING:
4 ounces Chinese white
  cabbage
2 ounces braised bamboo
  shoots (available canned)
1 scallion
2 tablespoons vegetable oil
2 tablespoons snow pickle,
  coarsely chopped

1½ tablespoons Sichuan Ja
  Tsai pickle, coarsely
  chopped
1½ tablespoons soy sauce
½ teaspoon sugar
1 tablespoon sesame oil
2 tablespoons watercress
  leaves, coarsely chopped, or
  coriander leaves (optional)

Cut the cabbage into ½-inch slices, the braised bamboo shoots into shreds (cut shreds again into ½-inch sections), and the scallion into ¼-inch pieces.

Heat the vegetable oil in a small frying pan or wok. When hot, add the braised bamboo shoots and the pickles. Stir them over medium heat for 1 minute. Add the cabbage and continue to stir-fry for 2½ minutes. Add the soy sauce, sugar, sesame oil, scallion, and watercress or coriander. Stir-fry them all together for 1½ minutes. Transfer to a glass basin or bowl to cool. When cold, put in the refrigerator to cool further for 1½ hours.

Divide the dough in two. Roll each half into sausage-shaped rolls 10–11 inches long. Cut each roll into disks approximately 1 inch thick. Flatten the disks with your palm and press them into pancakes 4–5 inches in diameter, making them slightly thicker in the center than at the rim.

Place a heaped tablespoon of the filling at the center of each thick pancake. Lift and flute the sides of the pancake firmly around the filling, puckering and gathering the rim up to cover the filling completely. When the rims meet at the top, close off by giving them a twirl and twist, and finally a pinch. Place these buns, puckered and twisted side down, on greaseproof paper in a warm spot for 45 minutes.

Turn the risen buns over and arrange them on top of a large heatproof plate covered with a damp cloth. Insert the plate and contents into a steamer and steam vigorously for 20 minutes. Allow the buns to stand for a couple of minutes before removing from the steamer. These buns can be eaten hot (preferably) or cold. When cold they can be reheated by placing them in a steamer for 6–7 minutes.

## STUFFED DUMPLINGS

In China dumplings are seldom served as solid balls of dough as they often are in the West; they are almost invariably prepared and cooked as stuffed dumplings, which consist of savory fillings wrapped in dough sheets that are made by mixing flour with hot water (if the dumplings are meant to be steamed) or cold water (if they are meant to be boiled). The usual proportion for 18–24 dumplings is to mix one portion (or cup) of water to 2½ portions of all-purpose flour.

To prepare the dough wrappers, first place the flour in a large mixing bowl. Make a well in the center and add water very gradually.

Start by adding just one third of the water and stir to make a firm dry dough. Add more water slowly and continue to stir until the two ingredients are thoroughly mixed. It is important to add water gradually, as more water can always be added as you go along. Knead the dough in the bowl for 3–4 minutes, and leave it to stand for 20 minutes to allow the dough to rise. Turn the dough out onto a lightly floured surface and knead for another 5 minutes. Divide the dough into two portions. Rest one portion in the bowl, and cover with a damp cloth. Make the other half into a large sausage-shaped roll about 12 inches long. Cut the roll into a dozen disks 1 inch thick. Use your hand and palm to flatten the disks, and roll each one with a small rolling pin into a pancake wrapper approximately 2½ inches in diameter and ⅛ inch thick. Give the pancake a quarter turn each time you roll, to keep it as round as possible.

Place a tablespoon of filling in the center of the pancake. Turn down and fold over the top two-fifths of the wrapper to barely cover the filling. Bring up the lower edge of the dough, pleating it slightly as you do so, and pinching the two edges together with thumb and finger to close and seal the dumpling. Repeat the process until all the dumplings are made. Arrange them on a floured tray while you wait to bring 1½–2 quarts of water to boil in a large saucepan.

There are three ways in which these dumplings are cooked: they can be water-boiled, steamed, or half boiled and half shallow-fried.

Most common is the "water-boiling" method. Put the dumplings in the large pan of boiling water and cover. When the contents return to a boil pour in a cup or small bowl of cold water. Replace the lid and wait for the contents to boil again. When this happens remove the lid and pour in another cup of cold water. Repeat this procedure three times, after which the dumplings should be cooked and normally float up to the top. Remove them with a perforated spoon.

These boiled dumplings are usually served with three types of dip sauces (soy sauce, chili oil or chili sauce, and shredded ginger in vinegar), which are placed on the table for the diners to dip their dumplings in. These simple dumplings are often eaten as bulk food in north China, and people think nothing of eating twenty to thirty of them at a meal at a time, but in the south they are eaten in much smaller quantities as snacks.

These dumplings can also be steamed by arranging them on top of a large heatproof plate covered with a damp cloth and steaming them vigorously for 18–20 minutes.

The third way of cooking these dumplings, a method peculiar to Beijing, is to part boil and part fry the dumplings. The usual way of doing this is to heat a heavy frying pan or skillet over high heat. When very hot add 3–3½ tablespoons of oil to heat in the pan for 30 seconds. Swirl the oil around until the surface of the pan or skillet is evenly greased. Reduce heat to medium-low. Add all the dumplings, crowding them together; tilt the pan so that its sides and the sides of the outer dumplings are well greased. Add 2 tablespoons of oil to a cup of boiling water. Stir them together and pour them evenly over the dumplings. The contents will start boiling and frothing. Shake the pan so that any dumplings that are slightly stuck to the side or bottom will loosen. Cover the pan with a lid and cook steadily for 5–6 minutes. Uncover the lid, shake the dumplings, and see how much water there is still in the pan. Raise the heat to allow the water to evaporate more quickly. Once the water has almost completely evaporated, turn off the heat altogether. Use a spatula or perforated spoon to remove the dumplings. Arrange them on a well-heated dish and serve them with same dip sauces as for the boiled dumplings. They are a great source of satisfaction to all those who appreciate Peking cuisine.

## SCALLION CAKES

The two most popular pancakes are these scallion cakes (or onion cakes) and sesame cakes. They are simple to make and, although very much a food of the masses, are regarded with nostalgia by many Chinese.

Scallion cakes are enjoyable to eat both because of their aromatic quality and because of their slight saltiness. They are usually eaten on their own, but of course they also go very well with savory foods, especially crunchy stir-fried vegetable dishes.

Makes 10

| | |
|---|---|
| 1 pound all-purpose flour | 2 teaspoons coarse-grain sea |
| ¼ teaspoon baking powder | salt or kosher salt |
| ½ teaspoon sugar | 5 scallions, coarsely chopped |
| ½ cup warm water | 5–6 tablespoons vegetable oil |

Place the flour in a mixing bowl. Sprinkle evenly with the baking powder and sugar. Mix with a wooden spoon. Add the water gradually, stirring and mixing with the wooden spoon. Knead the dough for 3–4 minutes. Cover it with a damp cloth and leave for half an hour, then knead again for 2–3 minutes. Divide the dough into ten portions and form into narrow strips 8–10 inches long. Flatten the strips with a rolling pin into ten bands of pancake thickness. Sprinkle each band first with salt and then with chopped scallions. Roll the bands lengthwise into long double-thickness spaghetti-shaped strips. Hold one end of the strip and turn the other end around in circles until the concentric rings form themselves around the center into a spiral pancake. Flatten the pancake with the palm of the hand. Repeat until the dough has been made into ten spiral pancakes.

Heat the oil on the bottom of a large flat-bottomed frying pan. When hot, lift the handle of the frying pan so that the surface of the pan is evenly greased. Place the spiral pancakes on the surface of the pan. Fry over low heat for 2½–3 minutes and turn the pancakes over. Repeat and fry gently until the pancakes are evenly browned on both sides.

## SESAME CAKES

These sesame cakes can be eaten on their own, or they can be served with savory foods. They are made from the same dough as is used for the scallion cakes in the previous recipe, except that no sugar and only half the salt is added. The dough is simply divided into ten portions and patted into round cakes ¼ inch thick. The top of each cake is then pressed onto a trayful of sesame seeds, leaving each one thickly covered. These cakes are then toasted, seed side down, on the hot surface of a dry griddle until they are well browned. They are then turned over to brown on the other side. For best results, they should be put into an oven preheated to 350°F to bake for 2–3 minutes before serving.

## EGG ROLLS

Makes 15–20

Egg rolls are one of the most commonly served items of food in Chinese restaurants in the West. The wrappers for them are best bought, as they are widely available from Chinese foodstores and supermarkets in packs of 50 sheets. They can be stored for a considerable length of time in the refrigerator. There remains only the filling to cook.

6–7 large Chinese dried
   mushrooms
3 scallions
3½ tablespoons vegetable oil
2 slices ginger root, shredded

3 ounces celery, shredded
2 ounces young carrots,
   shredded
1 teaspoon salt
1 teaspoon sugar

a pinch of pepper
3 ounces bean sprouts
1 tablespoon light soy sauce

3 teaspoons cornstarch
blended in 2 tablespoons
water
1–2 eggs, beaten

Soak the mushrooms in hot water for half an hour and drain. Remove and discard the stems and cut the caps into shreds. Cut the scallions into 1-inch sections.

Heat the oil in the frying pan or wok. When hot, add the mushrooms, ginger, celery, and carrots. Stir-fry over high heat for 2½ minutes. Add the salt, sugar, and pepper and continue to stir-fry for 1 minute. Add the sprouts and soy sauce and stir for a further 1½ minutes. Add the blended cornstarch and stir until all the vegetables are well coated with the sauce and more than half of the liquid has evaporated. Remove the contents and place in a bowl to cool. When completely cold the filling will be ready to use to stuff the pancakes.

The pancake wrappers are dough sheets measuring about 4 by 4 inches square. Place 2 tablespoons of the cooked filling along a line for about 2½ inches across the middle of the wrapper (between two corners). Bring up the bottom corner and fold over to cover the filling, and then bring in the corners from the two sides, which should nearly meet in the middle. Finally, bring down the top corner and roll the package over into a firm roll (like a large sausage roll) and close by wetting the last corner with a small amount of beaten egg. Rest the pancake roll on top of the last corner while you stuff the remaining rolls.

Deep-fry the pancake rolls in moderately hot oil for 6–7 minutes, or until golden brown and crispy. They can be eaten with or without dipping sauces (such as soy or soy and chili), but they must be consumed hot and crispy.

# SPRING ROLLS

These spring rolls are seldom eaten in the West but are served in China to welcome the advent of spring. They are not deep-fried; the same kind of pancake wrappers are used as for the egg rolls, but here they are simply heated on a griddle for 2–3 minutes on either side and then wrapped around a small quantity of quick-fried shredded vegetables. These vegetables can vary in number from two or three to half a dozen. They are just lightly quick-fried so that they retain most of their crispiness and are used in conjunction with two or more dipping sauces. The following are typical vegetables used in these rolls. The quantities given should be sufficient to stuff 20–30.

3–4 ounces bean sprouts
2 tablespoons ginger root, finely shredded
4 tablespoons vegetable oil
1 teaspoon salt
1½ tablespoons light soy sauce
3–4 ounces Chinese white cabbage, shredded

2 tablespoons Sichuan Ja Tsai pickle, finely shredded
1 tablespoon yellow bean sauce
3–4 ounces celery, shredded
3–4 ounces white button mushrooms, shredded
3–4 ounces young carrots, shredded
1 tablespoon sesame oil

The bean sprouts and ginger should be stir-fried together over high heat for 1½ minutes with one third of the seasonings. The same applies to the shredded cabbage and Ja Tsai pickle. The remaining oil, seasonings, and sauce should be used to stir-fry the celery, mushrooms, and carrots for about 2½ minutes. These three separately stir-fried collections of vegetables should be contained in separate serving dishes and grouped at the center of the dining table for the diners to stuff and fill their own pancakes with. Dishes or small bowls of dipping sauces should also be provided and should consist of good quality soy sauce, chili sauce, vinegar with shredded ginger, and yellow bean sauce with sugar and sesame oil (mix together 4 tablespoons yellow bean sauce, 2 tablespoons sugar, 1 tablespoon vegetable oil, ½ tablespoon sesame oil, and 3 tablespoons water, and stir over a moderate heat in a small saucepan for 3–4 minutes until consistent).

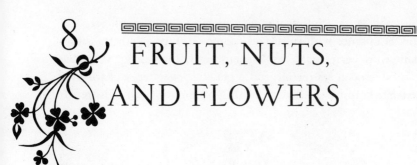

# 8
# FRUIT, NUTS, AND FLOWERS

Although fruits are eaten widely in China, we do not necessarily end our meals with a sweet dessert. Sweet dishes, however, are often used as side dishes, or pauses, in the long march of a multi-course Chinese meal, during which a diner may feel almost overwhelmed by the continuation of hot savoriness, despite its subtle nuances and variations. The occasional interjection of a fresh, pure, fruity, refreshing sensation is often very welcome.

On the other hand, there are also fruit soups and fruit gruels, sweet nut soups, and bean soups, which are drunk, like hot cocoa, for warmth and comfort. Many such items are combination dishes in which the inherent flexibility of Chinese food preparation comes into full play. This enables almost any number of dishes to be created, along the lines of the dried with the fresh, the juicy with the nutty, the sweet with the less sweet, and so on. The majority of these, especially the drier dishes, can be garnished or decorated with flowers.

Partly because of the frequent presence of sweetness in a large number of savory dishes, sweet-tasting fruits with a firm texture, such as apples, pears, melon, and pineapple, can often be cut into the same shape and size as the principal ingredient and incorporated into stir-fried or quick-braised dishes without disturbing their character; or in some cases they may be incorporated in the longer-cooked soy-braised dishes by adding them to the pot or pan during the later stages of cooking. For instance, shredded pears can be mixed into most hot-tossed and cold-tossed noodles (pages 151–55), or into Stir-fried Bean Sprouts with Garlic and Scallions (page 72); and apples can easily be incorporated into most hot and sour or sweet and sour dishes. Chunky-cut apples can be incorporated and cooked in a dish of Four Soy-braised Chunky Vegetables with Pickles (page 87), or even into a dish of Sichuan Hot-braised Stir-fried Eggplant (page 88). Many palates find the combination of sweet and hot flavors an appealing sensation. But it is when fresh fruits are cut into small pieces and combined with nuts and dried fruits and a basic food such as rice that the greatest range of dishes begins to emerge. The Chinese cookery custom of combining the sweet with the salty and savory makes it particularly exciting.

## SWEET FRIED RICE WITH CHERRIES

This dish is only mildly sweet and can be eaten with other salty and savory dishes. The large mound of fried rice, studded with red cherries and speckled with the green of scallions, looks very attractive and is also appealing to many palates.

Serves 4–5

| | |
|---|---|
| 2 scallions | 1 pound cooked rice |
| 1–2 salt eggs | ½ teaspoon salt |
| 1 medium-sized onion | 1 tablespoon sugar |
| 7–8 medium-sized cherries | 1½ tablespoons light soy |
| 2–3 eggs | sauce |
| 4 tablespoons vegetable oil | 2 tablespoons vegetarian stock |
| 3 teaspoons capers | 1 tablespoon butter or |
| 4–5 tablespoons canned corn | margarine |
| kernels | |

Chop the scallions into ¼-inch shavings, separating the white part from the green. Roughly chop the salt eggs and onion. Remove the pits from the cherries. Beat the eggs lightly.

Heat 3 tablespoons of the oil in a frying pan or wok. Add the onion and the white part of the scallions. Stir them in the hot oil for 1½ minutes. Add the salt eggs and capers, continue to stir for 1 minute, then push the ingredients to one side of the pan or wok. Add the remaining tablespoon of oil to the other side of the pan and pour in the beaten egg. When the eggs are about to set, add the corn. When the eggs have completely set, reduce the heat and scramble the contents together. When they are well mixed, push them to the side. Pour the cooked rice into the center and stir and mix it in with all the other ingredients. Sprinkle with the salt, sugar, soy sauce, and stock. Continue to turn and stir until all the ingredients are well mixed. Add the butter or margarine, the scallion greens, and the cherries and toss together with the other ingredients. Cook over low heat for 1 more minute. Turn the contents out onto a large, well-heated serving dish.

## FRIED RICE WITH BRAISED BAMBOO SHOOTS, CARROTS, GREEN PEAS, CHERRY TOMATOES, VIOLETS, AND NASTURTIUMS

An uncommonly attractive dish, which is equally satisfying to consume.

Serves 4–5

1 medium-sized onion
2 scallions

3 ounces braised bamboo
  shoots (available canned)
3 ounces braised carrots

2 tablespoons soy sauce
½ tablespoon sugar
2 tablespoons snow pickle
3 eggs
4–5 tablespoons cherry
  tomatoes

5–6 tablespoons vegetable oil
1 pound cooked rice
4–5 tablespoons green peas
1 tablespoon butter
½ handful of violet and
  nasturtium petals

Cut the onion into very thin slices, and the scallions, bamboo shoots, and carrots into ¼-inch pieces. Braise the carrots in 1½ tablespoons oil for 1½ minutes, add 2 tablespoons soy sauce and ½ tablespoon sugar, heat gently for 3 minutes, and drain. Coarsely chop the snow pickle. Lightly beat the eggs in a bowl. Cut the tomatoes into halves.

Heat 3 tablespoons oil in a frying pan or wok. When hot, add the onion and stir for 1½ minutes. Add the bamboo shoots and continue to stir for 1 minute. Then push them to one side of the pan or wok. Add 1 tablespoon oil to the other side of the pan or wok, followed by the eggs. Reduce the heat to allow the eggs to set slowly. When the eggs have set, scramble them with the other ingredients and push them to the sides of the pan or wok. Pour the rice into the center. Bring in the ingredients from the sides and scramble them together with the rice. Cook gently for 1 minute. Add the tomatoes, braised carrots, peas, butter, and chopped snow pickle, and sprinkle with the chopped scallions. Stir, turn, and mix all the ingredients together and cook for another minute.

Turn the contents of the pan or wok out onto a well-heated serving dish, heaping it up in a mound. Sprinkle and surround it with violets and nasturtiums and serve.

## FRIED RICE WITH PEANUTS, RADISHES, DICED PRESSED BEAN CURD, YELLOW RAISINS, SOY EGGS, APPLES, AND JASMINE BUDS

This grand mixture of fried rice, representing a wide variety of textures, flavors, and colors, is a substantial dish suitable for a family dinner, but it would also be an attractive dish to present at a dinner party. Although sugar is added, it is not quite a sweet dish, for it contains quite an element of saltiness. It could be described as a "sweet and salt" dish.

Serves 4–5

| | |
|---|---|
| 1 medium-sized onion | 1 teaspoon salt |
| 2 soy eggs | 1 pound cooked rice |
| 2–3 ounces seasoned pressed bean curd | 2 tablespoons yellow raisins |
| 1 medium-sized red apple | 1½ tablespoons butter |
| 3 eggs | 3 tablespoons green peas |
| 4 tablespoons small radishes | 2 teaspoons sugar |
| 4 tablespoons vegetable oil | 2 tablespoons light soy sauce |
| 3 tablespoons salted peanuts | ½ handful jasmine buds |
| | 1 teaspoon sesame oil |

Cut the onion into very thin slices. Cut the soy eggs, pressed bean curd, and apple (including the skin) into ¼-inch cubes. Beat the eggs lightly. Coarsely chop the radishes.

Heat 3 tablespoons of the oil in a frying pan or wok. When hot, add the onion and stir-fry for 1 minute. Add the peanuts, pressed bean curd, radishes, and salt. Stir-fry for 2 minutes and push them to one side of the pan or wok. Add the remaining oil to the other side of the pan. After 15–20 seconds pour in the beaten egg. Reduce the heat and wait until the eggs have set completely before scrambling them with all the other ingredients. Push the scrambled ingredients to the sides of the pan or wok. Pour the rice into the center, gradually bring in the ingredients from the sides, and stir and mix them evenly with the rice. Cook over low heat for 1 minute. Add the yellow raisins, butter, peas, soy eggs, and apple. Sprinkle with sugar and soy sauce. Turn and toss all the ingredients together until they are evenly mixed.

Turn the contents out onto a large serving dish, heaping it all up in one mound. Sprinkle with a handful of jasmine buds and the sesame oil and serve.

# SWEET RICE GRUELS AND SWEET SOUPS

Many of the following recipes illustrate the central position that rice occupies in Chinese food, whether sweet or savory, vegetarian or otherwise. It is probable that these rice dishes, sweetened and cooked with fruits, have evolved through convenience. Since rice is readily available in the Chinese kitchen and is neutral in taste, it can combine just as well with sweet ingredients and fruits as with meats, vegetables, and savories. The rice normally used in sweet dishes is glutinous rice, which has a shorter and rounder grain than the long-grain and oval-grain varieties.

Sweet soups occur frequently in the lengthy course of a Chinese dinner and are used to "punctuate" a sequence of savory dishes. They are thought to have a cleansing and refreshing effect on the palate before the diners embark on the second or third leg of savory dishes which a Chinese banquet or party dinner may well offer.

## SWEET RICE GRUEL WITH PRUNES AND PEARS

Like most of these dishes with a high sugar content, this is inclined to be very hot.

Serves 7–8

6–7 ounces glutinous rice
2 quarts water
5 tablespoons sugar
8 ounces canned prunes

3 medium-sized pears
3 tablespoons candied orange
  peel

Prepare the gruel first. Boil the rice in water, reduce the heat to very low, and simmer for 1½ hours. Add the sugar, prunes, and prune syrup. Peel and core the pears and cut them into ½-inch pieces. Roughly chop the orange peel. Bring the rice gruel to a boil again, add the pears and peel, and cook gently for 15 minutes.

Serve the gruel to the diners in small individual bowls, to be sipped and eaten slowly.

## SWEET RICE GRUEL WITH LOTUS NUTS AND CHINESE RED DATES

Serves 7–8

8 ounces Chinese red dates
6–7 ounces glutinous rice
2 quarts water
5 tablespoons sugar

8 ounces canned lotus nuts
2–3 tablespoons crystallized
  ginger, coarsely chopped

Bring the dates to a boil in a small saucepan of water and simmer gently for 35 minutes. Drain, seed, and chop the dates, cutting each one into quarters.

Prepare the rice gruel as in the previous recipe. When ready, add the dates and sugar and simmer together for 15 minutes. Add the drained lotus nuts and crystallized ginger and continue to simmer for 10 minutes. Serve to the diners individually in small bowls to be sipped and eaten slowly.

## SWEET RICE GRUEL WITH FRUIT AND NUTS

Serves 6–7

3–4 tablespoons dried figs
2–3 tablespoons crystallized
  ginger
6 medium-sized strawberries
2 slices pineapple
1 quart rice gruel (see page
  186)

4–5 tablespoons sugar
1½ tablespoons raisins
1½ tablespoons yellow raisins
4–5 tablespoons almonds or
  walnuts, coarsely chopped

Chop the figs and ginger the same size as the raisins. Cut the strawberries into halves, and the pineapple into ½-inch wedges.

Heat the rice gruel in a large saucepan. Add the crystallized ginger, pineapple pieces, figs, sugar, raisins, and nuts. Bring the contents to a boil and simmer gently for 25 minutes. Add the strawberries and simmer for 5 minutes. Serve in the same manner as in the two previous recipes.

187

## LOTUS NUT AND ORANGE TEA

This is one of the favorite sweet soups (here the word "tea," which is commonly used in China, is taken to mean "sweet soup"). The nutty, sesame taste of the dumplings provides a contrast to the sweet orange taste of the soup.

Serves 6–8

12 ounces canned lotus nuts
3 cups water
3–4 tablespoons sugar
6 oranges
2–3 tablespoons crystallized
   ginger

1½ tablespoons sesame paste
   or peanut butter
4–5 tablespoons rice flour
2 tablespoons cornstarch
   blended in 5 tablespoons
   water

Drain the lotus nuts, place them in a clean saucepan, and add the water and sugar. Bring to a boil and reduce heat to a simmer. Cook gently for 15 minutes. Meanwhile, peel the oranges, squeeze the juice from 3 of them, and chop the remaining 2 oranges into ¼-inch pieces. Chop the ginger into coarse grains. Add the sesame paste or peanut butter and 2½ tablespoons water to the rice flour in a mixing bowl. Mix and mash them together into a thick dough paste. Form the paste into 12–15 small dough balls or dumplings.

Put the dumplings into the saucepan in which the lotus nuts are simmering. When contents return to a boil, add the orange juice, chopped oranges, and ginger. Stir, and when the contents have come to a boil again stir in the blended cornstarch, which should thicken the soup. Cook for a further 1–2 minutes.

The "tea," or sweet soup, should be poured into a large serving bowl, then ladled out into small individual bowls for the diners to sip from—in small mouthfuls, as it is likely to be very hot.

## SWEET PEANUT SOUP WITH STRAWBERRIES OR CHERRIES

Serves 5–6

5 cups water
1½ teaspoons baking powder
12 ounces raw peanuts, shelled
1 tablespoon butter
4–5 tablespoons sugar

1½ tablespoons cornstarch dissolved in 4 tablespoons water
8 ounces small, fresh strawberries or cherries

Heat the water in an enamel saucepan. When warm, stir in the baking powder. Add the peanuts and bring to a boil. Reduce the heat, cover, and simmer gently for 1½ hours. Remove the lid and simmer for a further half hour. Add the butter, sugar, and cornstarch, and stir until they have completely dissolved.

Remove the stalks from the strawberries or pit the cherries and add to the pan. Stir well and simmer for 2 more minutes.

Serve in individual small bowls as a break in a sequence of savory dishes.

## SWEET LOTUS NUT SOUP WITH CHERRIES

Serves 5–6

1 quart water
1 teaspoon baking powder
10 ounces canned lotus nuts
1½ tablespoons cornstarch

blended in 4 tablespoons water
4–5 tablespoons sugar
1 tablespoon butter
8 ounces large cherries

189

Heat the water in an enamel saucepan. When warm, stir in the baking powder. Drain the lotus nuts and add them to the pan. Bring to a boil and simmer gently for 1 hour. Add the cornstarch, sugar, and butter. Stir until they have completely dissolved and the soup has thickened.

Remove the stalks and pit the cherries. Place 4–5 cherries at the bottom of each small serving bowl and pour in the sweetened lotus nut soup. Serve one bowl to each diner, either to conclude a meal or in the course of it to break the sequence of savory dishes.

## SWEET GINGER SOUP WITH DRIED LICHEES

Serves 5–6

3 cups water
4–5 tablespoons fresh ginger
  root, shredded
8 ounces dried lichees
4–5 tablespoons crystallized
  ginger

3–4 tablespoons sugar
1 tablespoon cornstarch
  blended in 3 tablespoons
  water

Heat the water in an enamel saucepan. Add the fresh ginger and bring to a boil. Reduce the heat and simmer for half an hour. Remove the ginger with a perforated spoon. Remove the shells of the dried lichees and add them to the pan to simmer for half an hour. Chop the crystallized ginger into quarter-sugar-lump-sized pieces and add them with the sugar to the pan. Stir in the blended cornstarch, which will thicken the soup.

Serve in small bowls to the individual diners. Small rose petals may be sprinkled on top of each bowl of soup to add color.

# SWEET GREEN PEA SOUP WITH LICHEES

Serves 5–6

| | |
|---|---|
| 1 pound dried green split peas | 1½ cups rice gruel (page 186) |
| 3 cups water | 4 tablespoons sugar |
| | 8 ounces canned lichees |

Soak the peas in water overnight. Bring to a boil in the same water. Simmer gently for 1½ hours. Add the rice gruel and stir in the sugar. Gently bring to a boil and continue to simmer for a further 20 minutes. Add the lichees, including their syrup, and bring to a boil once more. Stir, then serve by ladling into small bowls for individual diners, as in the previous recipes.

# SWEET RED BEAN SOUP WITH FRESH *LOONGNAN* FRUIT

During the summer, *loongnan*, or dragon's eyes, are grown and harvested in south China in greater profusion than lichees. They are therefore used extensively in numerous forms of sweet dishes.

Serves 5–6

| | |
|---|---|
| 12 ounces dried red beans | 12 ounces fresh or canned |
| 3 cups water | *loongnan* (available in |
| 1½ cups rice gruel (page 186) | Chinese foodstores) |
| 4–5 tablespoons sugar | |

Soak the beans in water overnight. Bring them to a boil in the same water. Simmer gently for 1¼ hours, uncovered. Add the rice gruel and stir in the sugar. Gently bring to a boil and simmer for 15 minutes. Add the shelled or skinned *loongnan* (including the syrup, if canned). Bring once more to a gentle boil. Stir and simmer for 10 minutes.

Serve by ladling into small individual bowls, as in the previous recipes.

## BAKED APPLES STUFFED WITH RED BEAN PURÉE

Serves 6

15 tablespoons red bean      6 medium-sized apples
purée: see below (or canned
red bean paste from
Chinese foodstores)

Sweet red bean purée can be made as follows: soak 1 pound dried red beans overnight in 1 quart water. Bring the water and beans to a boil in a deep casserole or enamel saucepan. Reduce the heat and simmer gently, uncovered, for 2 hours, until most of the water has evaporated. Put the softened beans and remaining water into a blender or food processor and purée. Return the bean purée to the casserole or saucepan and stir over low heat until the purée becomes much drier (about 20–30 minutes). Slowly add 4 tablespoons sugar and 6 tablespoons vegetable oil, stirring all the time to prevent burning. After 20 minutes, remove from the heat and allow the sweetened bean purée to cool. When cold, it should be ready for use as a filling to stuff the apples.

Cut a ½-inch slice horizontally off the top of each apple, retaining the slice to use as a lid. Core the apples and scoop out some of the pulp, leaving a wall ⅓ inch thick all around and at the base. Fill two-thirds of the cavity with the bean purée. Close the top of the cavity with the sliced apple top and secure it by inserting a toothpick.

Preheat the oven to 375°F. Fill a roasting pan with 2 inches of water. Stand the apples in the water and put the roasting pan in the oven to bake for 30 minutes. The apples should become quite tender and pleasant to eat in mouthfuls with the sweet filling.

## PEKING DUST

Peking Dust was a very popular dessert in Peking in the 1920s and 1930s, especially with the Western communities, who were enjoying their heyday in China's ancient capital.

Serves 4–5

1–1¼ pounds chestnuts
½ teaspoon salt
3–4 tablespoons sugar
1 cup heavy cream

2 tablespoons confectioners' sugar
4–5 rosebud sprigs with 1 or 2 leaves

Score the chestnuts with a crisscross cut on the flat side of each one. Drop into boiling water and cook for 45 minutes. Drain and shell the chestnuts. In a blender or food processor, purée the chestnut meat with the salt and sugar. Whip the cream with the confectioners' sugar.

Divide the chestnut mix into four or five portions and heap each portion into a mound at the center of a small dessert plate. Top each mound with 2–3 tablespoons of the sweetened whipped cream. Place a sprig of rosebud at the base of each mound of Peking Dust, half buried by it, as if it were a solitary bloom surviving unattended and uncared for in a corner of a desert.

## GLAZED HONEY BANANAS OR APPLES

The unusual sensation of crackling through the thin coating of crystallized sugar (like thin ice), which is highly sweet, and chewing and munching it with the softer ingredient of fried banana or apple underneath makes this a delicious dish. For decades now this has been one of the favorite desserts served in those Chinese restaurants in the West that specialize in Peking cuisine. This dish can be further enhanced by serving it with scoops of different-colored fruit sorbets, strewn with the petals of different-colored flowers.

Serves 4–6

4 medium-sized bananas, or 3
   medium-sized apples
3 tablespoons cornstarch
1 egg, lightly beaten
Oil for deep-frying

SYRUP:
7–8 tablespoons sugar
5–6 tablespoons water
3 tablespoons honey
3 tablespoons vegetable oil

Cut each banana into four equal pieces or each apple into eighths. Dip each piece of banana or apple first into the cornstarch and then into the beaten egg, coating each piece well.

Deep-fry the banana or apple pieces until slightly brown. Remove and drain on absorbent paper.

To prepare the syrup, mix the sugar, water, honey, and oil together in a small saucepan and cook over medium heat, stirring all the while, until the mixture begins to turn brown. Using chopsticks or tongs, dip each piece of fried banana or apple first into the syrup and then into a bowl of ice water. Remove immediately and drain on waxed paper or the lightly greased surface of a platter. The sudden dip into ice water crystallizes the coating, which will crack when bitten into.

When a sufficient number of banana or apple pieces have been dipped, crystallized, and drained, arrange them on a serving dish for the diners to help themselves.

# HARVEST EIGHT-TREASURE RICE PUDDING

This is a classic Chinese dessert that is frequently served during Chinese dinner parties or banquets. Surrounding the pudding with chrysanthemums, which begin to bloom during the early autumn, enhances the festive feeling associated with the harvest season.

Serves 8–10

3 tablespoons butter or margarine

5–6 tablespoons colored glacé fruit

2 tablespoons yellow raisins

2 tablespoons raisins

1½ cups glutinous rice

4 tablespoons sugar

2 tablespoons vegetable oil

1 cup sweet red bean purée (page 192)

5–6 tablespoons nuts: lotus nuts, melon-seed meats, peanuts, or walnuts

Rub the sides and bottom of a heatproof bowl generously with butter or margarine. Press on the glacé fruit and raisins in an artistic pattern so that they stick to the walls and base.

Prepare the rice by washing and boiling it in 1¼ times its own volume of water over very low heat for 15 minutes and leaving it to stand for a further ten minutes. Stir in the sugar and oil and mix evenly with the rice. Spread a layer of rice 1 inch thick evenly over the bottom and sides of the bowl, completely covering the glacé fruit and raisins, taking care not to knock any of them off. Spread a layer of red bean purée ½ inch thick over the rice on the bottom of the bowl. Add another layer of rice 1 inch thick to cover the bean purée. Sprinkle the top of the rice with the nuts and the melon-seed meats, then cover these with ½ inch of rice. Repeat the procedure until there are three seams of bean purée, rice, and nuts and melon seeds, ending up with a thick layer of rice, which should come to within ½ inch of the top of the bowl. Cover firmly with aluminum foil.

Insert the bowl with its contents into a steamer for 50–60 minutes. To unmold, carefully insert the blade of a knife all around the edge of the pudding, then put a large round serving dish over the top of the bowl and quickly and carefully invert it. To make this pudding even more colorful, surround it with small chrysanthemum blossoms.

# INDEX

## ABOUT THE AUTHOR

Kenneth Lo was born in Foochow, China, and was educated at the Universities of Peking, Cambridge, and London. Since arriving in England in 1936 he has been a diplomat, publisher of Chinese prints, industrial relations officer (with Chinese seamen in Liverpool), lecturer, journalist, BBC broadcaster and professional tennis player.

But Kenneth Lo is best known today as one of the world's authorities on Chinese cooking. He has written numerous successful books on Chinese cookery, including *Chinese Vegetarian Cooking* and *Chinese Regional Cooking*, also published by Pantheon.

Apart from writing about Chinese food and managing one of London's top Chinese restaurants, Kenneth Lo now runs a very successful multi-region Chinese cookery school. During 1982–83 two British television films were made of Kenneth Lo's activities.

However, the one activity that Kenneth Lo has pursued continuously throughout his life is tennis. He was a Chinese Davis Cup and Wimbledon player in 1946, and four decades later he was chosen to represent Great Britain in the Britannia Cup for Veterans and was selected to play again for Britain in the 1984 Crawford Cup for Superveterans.